Contents

RELIGIOUS SIGNING

Elaine Costello
Illustrated by Lois Lehman

BANTAM BOOKS
NEW YORK • TORONTO • LONDON • SYDNEY • AUCKLAND

RELIGIOUS SIGNING
A Bantam Book / April 1986

ISBN 0-553-34244-4

Published simultaneously in the United States and Canada

Bantam Books are published by Bantam Books, a division of Bantam
Doubleday Dell Publishing Group, Inc. Its trademark, consisting of the
words "Bantam Books" and the portrayal of a rooster, is Registered in U.S.
Patent and Trademark Office and in other countries. Marca Registrada.
Bantam Books, 1540 Broadway, New York, New York 10036.

PRINTED IN THE UNITED STATES OF AMERICA

To my wonderful parents, Rev. Alvin A. Walter and Ella Schiebel Walter, this book is most lovingly dedicated as a token of my esteem and in commemoration of their fiftieth wedding anniversary and of my father's fiftieth year in the ministry.

Acknowledgments

Collecting religious signs to represent different denominations involved the cooperation and expertise of many people. The selflessness of those who contributed and gave of their time is hereby documented in small recognition of their efforts. It is hoped that in return for their time and help they find this volume exactly what they hoped it would be and what they needed to assist them in their important work with deaf people.

Gina Bearden (Baptist)
Rev. Ray C. Bearden (Baptist)
Rev. Clifford Bruffey (Baptist)
Father Thomas Coughlin (Roman Catholic)
Rev. Don Chevalley (Baptist)
Rev. Jay L. Croft (Episcopal)
Alexander Fleischman (Jewish)
Rabbi Fred Friedman (Jewish)
Cynthia Gilmore (Assemblies of God)
Rev. Thomas J. Gilmore (Assemblies of God)

Nancy Grandel (Lutheran)
Sister Mary Ann Phelan, S.P. (Roman Catholic)
Rev. George Natonick (Lutheran)
Rev. Daniel Pokorny (Lutheran)
Rev. LeRoy E. Schauer (Methodist)
Dorothy J. Steffanic (Roman Catholic)
Patricia Stevens (Jewish)

My deepest appreciation is also here expressed to LuAnn Walther, my editor, who believed in me and without whose encouragement I would not have undertaken the creation of this book. Her sensitivity to the integrity of American Sign Language gave me the courage to compile this text regardless of the magnitude of the task.

Most particularly I am grateful to Lois Lehman, who has incredible skill in rendering drawings of signs from her native language. She consistently exhibits the highest level of professionalism in photographing the models and recording them with lifelike faithfulness and clarity.

Sign Models

Gina Bearden

Rev. Ray C. Bearden

Rev. Clifford Bruffey

Fr. Thomas Coughlin

Rev. Don Chevalley

Rev. Jay L. Croft

Alexander Fleischman

Rabbi Fred Friedman

Cynthia Gilmore

Rev. Thomas Gilmore

Nancy Grandel

Sr. Mary Ann Phelan

Rev. George Natonick

Rev. LeRoy Schauer

Dorothy J. Steffanic

Patricia Stevens

Introduction

Since its early use in Spanish monasteries where silence was prescribed for the monks but where manual communication was permitted, to an ever-increasing number of churches and synagogues providing services to deaf people today, sign language has played a major role in religious settings. It is thought that more hearing people develop a desire for learning sign language because of contact with deaf people or interpreters in religious services than as a result of any other influence. The large number of sign language classes conducted in religious buildings is partial evidence of this phenomenon.

The signs presented in this book have been collected from various denominations working with deaf people. The book does not purport to document all the variations of signs used to represent religious concepts. It is, however, an earnest attempt to compile those that are commonly used, along with an indication of their appropriate application.

Although this book may be used by both beginning and advance signers, it does not contain signs used in secular life. In order to converse in general terms wih deaf people, it will be necessary to supplement the religious sign vocabulary with the signs presented in my companion book, *Signing: How to Speak with Your Hands*. Incorporating the grammatical structure of American Sign Language with the sign vocabulary will result in mastering sign language as it is used by deaf people.

The Influence of the Church in Deaf Education

Ancient texts indicate that among the Egyptians as well as among the Greeks and later among the Romans, deaf people were denied the rights of inheritance, marriage, education, and even salvation. The exclusion of deaf people from religious rituals was more a result of ignorance about them than it was discrimination against them. The rabbis and priests could not communicate with deaf people, so they exempted them from religious responsibilities. The early efforts by parents to employ priests to teach their deaf children was an attempt to restore these rights to them.

The first recorded use of sign language was not among deaf people, but among hearing people. Monks, under vows of silence, used sign language in Cistercian monasteries as early as A.D. 328 and are still using it today, although the practice of silence has become somewhat relaxed. The number of signs used by the monks in the ancient Spanish monasteries seemed to vary from order to order, but by the eleventh century sign lists from different monasteries averaged about four hundred signs. The more signs recorded on a list from a monastery, the stricter the code of silence. These signs and their system of use differ greatly from the sign language used by deaf people. Nevertheless, it is certain that the monastic use of sign language had great influence on early attempts to teach deaf children through the signs.

A Spanish nobleman placed his two deaf sons in one of these Cistercian monasteries in 1545, presumably to prevent them from procreating and to put them out of sight. But there, one of the Benedictine monks, Pablo Ponce de León, began to teach the children about the doctrines of Christianity, thereby establishing the first school for the deaf. Little is known of Ponce de León's method, but it is said that he primarily used reading and writing to teach speech. It is also thought that he used a manual alphabet and signs, both drawn from the monastic environment. One of the boys died young, but the other learned to speak and sign in the monastery choir. As a result other deaf children of Spanish nobility were sent to Ponce de León for instruction.

About thirty years after the death of Ponce de León, Juan Pablo Bonet, another Spanish priest, published a book about teaching the deaf. In that book Bonet presented a system of training the deaf through the use of a one-handed manual alphabet. There is enough historical evidence to suggest that it was the same alphabet used by Ponce de León, and it is essentially the same manual alphabet used in the United States today.

The work among deaf children in Spain influenced the establishment of educational work among the deaf in France, although it lagged behind the Spanish work by about two hundred years. Jacob Rodrigues Périere, the first teacher of the deaf in France, was a Spanish native who migrated to France to escape religious persecution. Périere began first by teaching his own deaf sister, but after his reputation spread, he took on other pupils whom he taught to read, talk, lip-read, and use the manual alphabet.

The second leader in establishing educational practices in France was a Catholic monk, Abbé Charles Michel de l'Épée, who in the eighteenth century undertook the religious instruction of the two deaf daughters of one of his parishioners. Espousing the concept that sign language was the natural language of the deaf, Épée attempted to adapt the signs he found used by the deaf community in Paris to French syntax and morphology, not unlike the manual English systems used in the United States today. He also used the manual alphabet from Bonet's book and the articulation techniques that had been published in a Dutch text. Epée's techniques were so successful that his fame spread to other European countries, who sent educators to him for training so they could begin schools for the deaf in their own countries.

Épée's work was carried on by another French priest, Abbé Sicard, who moved educational practices toward a more natural use of sign language and its grammar. It was Sicard who taught the American clergyman Thomas Hopkins Gallaudet, who had been traveling throughout Europe seeking methods of instruction to use with the deaf in the United States, the French techniques. It is this French influence that is evident in the structure of American Sign Language today.

When Reverend Gallaudet returned to the United States, he brought with him a deaf French teacher, Laurent Clerc. The efforts of Gallaudet and Clerc resulted in the opening of the first permanent American school for the deaf in Hartford, Connecticut. As in Europe, religion was an important influence in the founding of this school. Reverend Gallaudet, an Episcopal minister, recorded the following in his diary at the beginning of his work: "O Almighty God, Thou knowest my desire to be devoted to Thy service and to be made the instrument of training the deaf and dumb for heaven."

In the fifty years following the opening of Gallaudet's school in 1817 eighteen schools for the deaf were founded and funded by state legislatures. Of these eighteen schools eight were begun under the leadership of a minister and two under sons of ministers.

Ministry to the Deaf in the United States

Deaf ministry among different denominations has taken on a number of forms. In most instances churches and synagogues provide sign language interpreters to sign church services and other religious ceremonies. Often the interpreters are volunteers or children of deaf parents. Generally such congregations have predominately hearing members, and the interpreter provides a vital link between the clergyman and the few deaf parishioners. Although this is an efficient way to reach both deaf and hearing members simultaneously, deaf people tend not to participate in other functions outside the regularly scheduled services since they cannot communicate freely with the other members. Some problems may also arise from issues of confidentiality in counseling sessions where an interpreter is used to assist the exchange between the clergyman and the deaf person.

To facilitate direct communication with their deaf members, many ministers and rabbis learn sign language themselves. In some denominations special training programs are available in the seminaries for students interested in future ministry to the deaf. More often clergy take sign language instruction after being assigned to a congregation having a few deaf members. As an even more effective measure to reach deaf people, deaf clergy have been ordained into almost every denomination. The Episcopal Church and the Methodist Church have particularly espoused this practice through the years, supporting their contention that a deaf minister is more capable of ministering to deaf people than a hearing minister because of a deeper understanding and rapport with them.

The following sections trace the history of religious ministry to deaf people in the United States among those denominations whose early efforts have developed into fairly extensive ministries. In addition to denominations covered in some depth, some notice should be made of other denominations with smaller, yet notable, ministries to deaf people. The Mennonite Church began its ministry to the deaf in 1911 and has concentrated its efforts in Pennsylvania and several northern states. The Church of Jesus Christ of Latter-Day Saints began its activities by teaching deaf children in 1896, later merging their educational program into the Utah State School for the Deaf. The church's present efforts now reach nineteen communities served by fifty-eight missionaries, half of whom are deaf themselves. The Assemblies of God Church established its first church for deaf members in 1929 in Los Angeles. Their evangelistic work among the deaf has expanded tremendously during the past fifty years. Presently the church supports eight ministers to the deaf and a large number of interpreters, who serve in three hundred forty churches across the country. The Church of Christ began its ministry to the deaf in Texas in 1935 and now has about one hundred interpreters. The independent Christian Church began its ministry to the deaf in Idaho in 1957, presently serving approximately eight congregations with ordained ministers and interpreters. Notably the Christian Church supports Deaf Missions in Council Bluffs, Iowa, whose goal is to prepare and distribute visual and printed materials for use in deaf ministries. Deaf Missions has recently undertaken the ambitious Omega Project, an effort to record the Bible in American Sign Language on videotape. The Presbyterian Church has been active in deaf ministry in a limited way since 1930, and in 1982 began formally to involve deaf people in church decisions that affect them.

Episcopal. The Episcopal Church was the first denomination to meet the religious needs of deaf people in the United States. The first known church services for the deaf were held in 1846 by the Protestant Episcopal Church in Philadelphia in what now is known as All Souls Church. Shortly after that Reverend Thomas Hopkins Gallaudet's eldest son, Thomas Gallaudet, began conducting services in sign language in New York city in what is now Saint Ann's Church for the Deaf. These two churches were the beginning of any extensive ministry of the Episcopal Church among the deaf.

The Episcopal Church has taken the leadership in installing deaf priests to the ministry. The first deaf man ever ordained to the ministry was Henry Winter Syle, who was admitted as a candidate for Holy Orders in 1875 amid considerable opposition from the bishops and priests of the Church. He advanced to the priesthood in 1883 and spent the next seven years before his premature death establishing many new programs and services for the Episcopal Church in Pennsylvania. Through the years approximately forty-five deaf men have been ordained to the priesthood of the Episcopal Church.

In 1972 the Episcopal Church established an umbrella organization for ministry to the deaf nationwide. That organization, now known as the Episcopal Conference of the Deaf, provides financial support to establish new programs within the church.

Roman Catholic. The Roman Catholic Church was the second religious body to administer specially to the needs of deaf people in the United States. Laurent Clerc, the deaf teacher whom Thomas Hopkins Gallaudet brought back from Europe with him to teach in the first school for the deaf in this country, was a Roman Catholic. However, shortly after arriving, Clerc left the Catholic faith, and Catholic clergy were not permitted to enter the school for the next eighty years.

The first Catholic school for the deaf was founded in 1839 by two Sisters of Saint Joseph from Lyons, France, who began the school in a convent in St. Louis, Missouri. That school continues to this day, almost one hundred fifty years later. The opening of the Saint Joseph's School for the Deaf was followed twenty years later by the opening of Saint Mary's School for the Deaf in Buffalo, New York, and ten more schools have been established since that time. The Roman Catholic Church has taken the leadership in establishing parochial schools for the deaf including establishing special classrooms for deaf children in their existing day schools since the early 1950s.

In terms of pastoral care, the Roman Catholic Church presently has more than one hundred full-time salaried ministers and approximately fifty part-time salaried ministers to the deaf assisted by another four hundred lay workers. More than half of the dioceses have salaried personnel to minister to their deaf parishioners. At the present time three deaf men have been ordained as priests, the first of whom, Father Thomas Coughlin, is a model for sign illustrations in this book.

Lutheran. The Lutheran Church–Missouri Synod (LC–MS) was the third denomination to take an active interest in the spiritual needs of deaf people. Its work began quite by accident when deaf children came for religious instruction to what was intended to be a new orphanage in Detroit. Instead the institution opened in 1874 as a school for the deaf. It was by special request of one of the graduates of this school that church services for deaf people were begun in 1894 at what is now Bethlehem Lutheran Church in Chicago. August P. Reinke was the first pastor to that congregation, and as his reputation regarding his ability to conduct church services in sign language spread, he was called upon to establish a regular circuit of preaching in various midwestern cities. Soon thereafter LC–MS officially recognized the mission work among the deaf and established a Deaf Mission Commission. Within the next five years the number of pastors serving deaf people grew to seven, and by the time LC–MS celebrated its fiftieth anniversary of working with the deaf, there were twenty pastors conducting church services in approximately two hundred seventy-five cities across the United States.

The Lutheran Church–Missouri Synod has developed the most extensive work of the three Lutheran synods, with special training programs in both of its seminaries for students wishing to study for the deaf ministry. At the present time there are approximately fifty full-time LC–MS pastors working with deaf people, a few of whom are deaf themselves. The pastors are organized for the purpose of mutual support and continued education into the Ephphatha Conference, which was founded in 1903 and continues to meet annually. The International Lutheran Deaf Association was organized to assist the LC–MS deaf ministry throughout the world. LC–MS supports two schools for the deaf, the original one in Detroit and another in Long Island, New York, which was opened in 1951.

A second Lutheran synod, the Lutheran Church in America (LCA), began its deaf ministry in 1889 at what is now the Mount Airy School for the Deaf in Pennsylvania, where an LCA pastor began giving religious instruction to the students. The work of LCA among the deaf has largely concentrated in the state of Pennsylvania over the years. A part-time office has been established to coordinate LCA's deaf ministry in the Central Pennsylvania Synod, but there is no national LCA office.

The deaf ministry of the third Lutheran synod, the American Lutheran Church (ALC), began with religious instruction of deaf children at the Minnesota State School for the deaf at Faribault in 1898. Similar to the growth of the LC–MS, ALC pastors began conducting services on an itinerant basis across the upper Midwest. The pastors were organized under the Ephphatha Missions to the Deaf and Blind giving synodical support. The first ALC church especially for deaf members was the Bread of Life Lutheran Church for the Deaf founded in 1950 in Minneapolis. At the present time ALC maintains a full-time home office with responsibility for the church's work with all disabled people. It has four full-time and one hundred sixteen pastors working primarily in interpreted services.

Methodist. The fourth religious body to begin work among deaf people was the Methodist Church. Beginning in 1890 Philip J. Hasenstab, a deaf teacher from the Illinois School for the Deaf in Jacksonville, made monthly trips to Chicago to conduct services for the deaf community. Three years later he left teaching and became a full-time pastor of the Chicago Mission for the Deaf. Hasenstab was the first of a large number of deaf men who have been ordained into the Methodist ministry through the years supporting the church's contention that a deaf minister has a deeper understanding of the problems and needs of deaf people.

Shortly after the founding of the Chicago mission, three more Methodist missions were started in Baltimore, Cincinnati, and Florida. At the present time the United Methodist Church has more than fifteen organized ministries especially for deaf people and many more interpreted services for deaf people who attend churches whose members are predominantly hearing.

In 1977 the United Methodist Congress of the Deaf was organized with the primary purpose of building support systems for hearing-impaired Methodist members. It also develops religious curriculum materials and advances an awareness among hearing churches regarding deaf persons.

Baptist. After the turn of the century the Southern Baptist Convention, the most active Baptist fellowship working among the deaf, began conducting religious services for the deaf. The work began under the leadership of a deaf man, John Michaels, principal of the Arkansas School for the Deaf, who traveled from city to city organizing Sunday School classes for deaf people. His work and that of a deaf woman who went to Cuba in 1902 to provide religious instruction were the first two missionary activities of the Southern Baptist Convention under its Home Mission Board. From these beginnings the work of the Southern Baptist Convention has grown to thirty-eight churches especially for deaf people and about eight hundred other churches with special arrangements for deaf people to participate in their services and programs. The most common arrangement is to have lay workers assist the minister in providing Sunday School classes training union, or special Bible study groups. More than one thousand interpreters are in their employment to assist deaf people in participating in the activities of hearing members of the congregations.

There are a number of Baptist fellowships actively involved in work with deaf parishioners. One group, the Independent Baptist Church, has a sizable number of hearing and deaf ministers, lay ministers, and interpreters. It supports a school for deaf children, a high school, and even a college-degree program. One of its largest programs is a camp founded in 1950 by Dr. and Mrs. Bill Rice in Murfreesboro, Tennessee, for the purpose of providing spiritual training for deaf people. As a result of programs to more than one thousand campers annually, more than eight hundred Sunday School classes for deaf children have been begun both in the United States and abroad.

Jewish. Around the turn of the century deaf Jews organized themselves into Hebrew associations to provide a place for members to meet for social and religious activities. New York City, the port of arrival for many Jewish immigrants, was the primary headquarters for such associations. The Hebrew Association of the Deaf and the New York Society of the Deaf, founded in 1907 and 1911 respectively, were two of the earliest associations and are still presently active. They were followed by similar associations in Philadelphia, Baltimore, Cleveland, and Los Angeles.

The National Congress of Jewish Deaf was established in 1956 and served as a clearinghouse of information about religion, education, and culture for approximately 170,000 hearing-impaired Jews in all branches of Judaism. Alexander Fleischman, who served as a model for this book, is the present executive director.

A major concern in the Jewish faith, just as in other religions, is to encourage rabbis to work with deaf people and for rabbinical seminaries to admit deaf candidates. With increased numbers of men and women becoming ordained into the rabbinate for work with the deaf, deaf people now have the opportunity to participate in Jewish religious observances in most major cities. Only recently the first deaf rabbi, Rabbi Fred Friedman—a sign model in this book—was ordained in Baltimore. He is one of six regional representatives across the nation for Our Way, the outreach program for Jewish deaf of all ages of the National Conference of Synagogue Youth.

Signing in Religious Settings

Signs used for religious services and ceremonies are closely aligned with the particular doctrines of the faith represented. One must be very careful in choosing a particular sign or variation for an English gloss. In fact, it may often be better to use a string of signs to explain the sign's meaning rather than choose one sign, thus assuring that the concept is clearly and conceptually presented. This cautionary note is not meant to deter the beginner from learning religious signs, but rather to exercise somewhat more sensitivity in the selection of signs than one normally would with secular signs with generic references.

Religious signs are usually formed larger and more dramatically than when used in a personal conversation. Signs that traditionally may be formed with one hand are often rendered with two hands—CELEBRATE and HONOR, for example. One of the reasons for these enlarged movements is for clarity when leading a congregation. The exaggerated signs, when performed smoothly, are especially beautiful in the "singing" of hymns.

Many religious signs are iconic, that is, they resemble some aspect of the object or character of the object they represent. For example, the sign CROWN looks very much like the hands are holding a crown and placing it on the head. In this book the text accompanying each drawing brings these mnemonic clues to the reader's attention to help him or her recall the sign. The text may also indicate the appropriate usage of that sign in a religious setting.

Many religious signs are also initialized, that is, the hands are formed like the fingerspelled first letter of the English gloss for that sign. Initialized signs are often used to differentiate between the literal meanings of a sign that may have originally had several English glosses. LAW, COMMANDMENT, HALACHA, and TESTAMENT, for example, have some similarities in meaning, but the initialized handshapes distinguish them from one another for precision in communication. In this book signs that are formed in a similar manner but with different initialized handshapes are cross-referenced next to the drawings. Learning these similarly formed signs together sometimes helps in remembering them.

The signs in this book are more nationally representative than the models' current home addresses might indicate. Because ministers, priests, and rabbis tend to travel from region to region to attend conferences and are often reassigned to different parishes or communities, the signs in this book are, for the most part, being used nationally.

It is hoped that this volume will help the process of identifying those signs fledgling congregations and others serving in a ministry to deaf people find most applicable for their use. One must keep in mind that deaf people themselves do not necessarily know or use all of the religious signs contained in this book any more than a hearing person automatically knows or uses all of the words in a dictionary.

The Signs in This Book

The signs in this book were collected from interviews with deaf and hearing ministers, priests, rabbis, laypeople, and interpreters who shared their expertise with a common sense of dedication and cooperation. In each case the interviewed person seemed to be cognizant of the book's goal: to present widely accepted signs that appropriately represented each denomination's doctrines. In the case of minor variations of the signs suggested by different informants, this book illustrates the most common sign and notes the variation in the text under the drawing. If sign variations seemed quite diverse but widely used, they were included in the book as alternates.

Sign variations are probably more prevalent in the use of religious signs than with a more general vocabulary. The reason for these variations is that each religious denomination has terminology unique to the doctrines taught within that church. The doctrines must often be understood before the concepts can be transliterated into sign language. Because there have been no comprehensive books of signs for use in religious settings, interpreters unfamiliar with the terminology and doctrines have often been unable to select appropriate strings of signs or equivalent signs for the concepts in sermons, liturgies, religious ceremonies, and hymns. As a result the interpreters have developed "impromptu" signs to facilitate expressing often repeated terms. After frequent use the impromptu signs may have been adopted by the members of that congregation and after time may have spread within the region or denomination.

Most of the illustrations in this book are presented from the front view of the signer. This means that the illustrations show a right-handed signer, and the descriptions are written for persons with a right-handed dominance. Left-handed signers should reverse the signs.

Lois Lehman's illustrations in the book use multiple images along with arrows to describe the sign formation and movement as accurately as possible. To keep the drawings uncluttered a simple system was used: ① and ② indicate the sequence in which the parts of a compound sign are formed, and Ⓐ and Ⓑ indicate a change of hand position in a sign. The written explanation specifies whether the sign movements should be repeated or if the hands alternate in producing it.

You will note that many signs include the notation "Add the person marker." The marker is formed by bringing both flat hands, palms facing inwards, down along the side of the body. This marker is sometimes used to designate an occupation such as PREACHER or nationality such as AMERICAN.

Good luck with your signing. You will find deaf people to be patient and willing to assist you in your efforts. Use every opportunity to practice your skills with deaf people and observe firsthand the richness of this unique language, which uses space and movement for the purpose of communication.

Executive Offices for Religious Organizations

Anabaptist Deaf Ministries
P.O. Box 247
Riverdale, MD 20738

Baptist Sunday School Board Special Ministries
127 Ninth Avenue North
Nashville, TN 37234

Catholic Charities Office for Disabled Persons
Deafness Services
191 Joralemon Street
Brooklyn, NY 11201

Catholic Deaf Apostolate
243 Steele Road
West Hartford, CT 06117

Cave Spring United Methodist Church
Ministries to Deaf Children
P.O. Box 305
Cave Spring, GA 30124

Central Bible College
3000 North Grant Avenue
Springfield, MO 65803

Christian Record Services
Division for the Deaf
4444 South 52nd Street
P.O. Box 6097
Lincoln, NE 68506

Christian Reform Church
Committee on Disability Concerns
2850 Kalamazoo Avenue SE
Grand Rapids, MI 49560

Christians for the Liberation of the Deaf Community
2421 Perry Street NE
Washington, DC 20018

Deaf International Bible College
800 South Tenth Street, Suite 5
Minneapolis, MN 55404

Deaf International Correspondence Institute
2557 West San Juan Street
Coupeville, WA 98239

Deaf Ministries Worldwide
P.O. Box 985
Sulphur, OK 73086

Deaf Missions
RR2, Box 26
Council Bluffs, IA 51503

Ephphatha Services
Ministry with Persons with Disabilities
422 South Fifth Street
Minneapolis, MN 55415

Episcopal Conference of the Deaf
1616 Calle Santiago
Pleasanton, CA 94566

Evangelical Lutheran Church of America
Ministry with Disabilities
8765 West Higgins Road
Chicago, IL 60631

General Council of the Assemblies of God
Deaf Culture Ministries
1445 Boonville Avenue
Springfield, MO 65802

Home Mission Board of the Southern Baptist Convention
Language Church Extension Division
1350 Spring Street NW
Atlanta, GA 30367

International Catholic Deaf Association
8002 South Sawyer Road
Darien, IL 60561

International Lutheran Deaf Association
1333 South Kirkwood Road
St. Louis, MO 63122

Lutheran Church Missouri Synod
Mission to the Deaf and Blind
1333 South Kirkwood Road
St. Louis, MO 63122

Mennonite Board of Missions
Office of Deaf Ministries
P.O. Box 370
Elkhart, IN 46515

Mill Neck Services for Deaf Adults
Frost Mill Road
P.O. Box 193
Mill Neck, NY 11765

National Catholic Office for Persons with Disabilities
P.O. Box 29113
Washington, DC 20017

National Catholic Office for the Deaf
814 Thayer Avenue
Silver Spring, MD 20910

National Congress of Jewish Deaf
c/o Judy Slomovic Gunter
198-3 Crittenden Way
Rochester, NY 14623

National Council of Churches of Christ
Deaf Ministry Committee
P.O. Box 247
Riverdale, MD 20738

National Deaf Culture Fellowship
800 South Tenth Street, Suite 4
Minneapolis, MN 55404

Our Way—NCSY
45 West 36th Street
New York, NY 10018

United Methodist Church
Health and Welfare Ministries Program
475 Riverside Drive, Room 350
New York, NY 10115

The Manual Alphabet

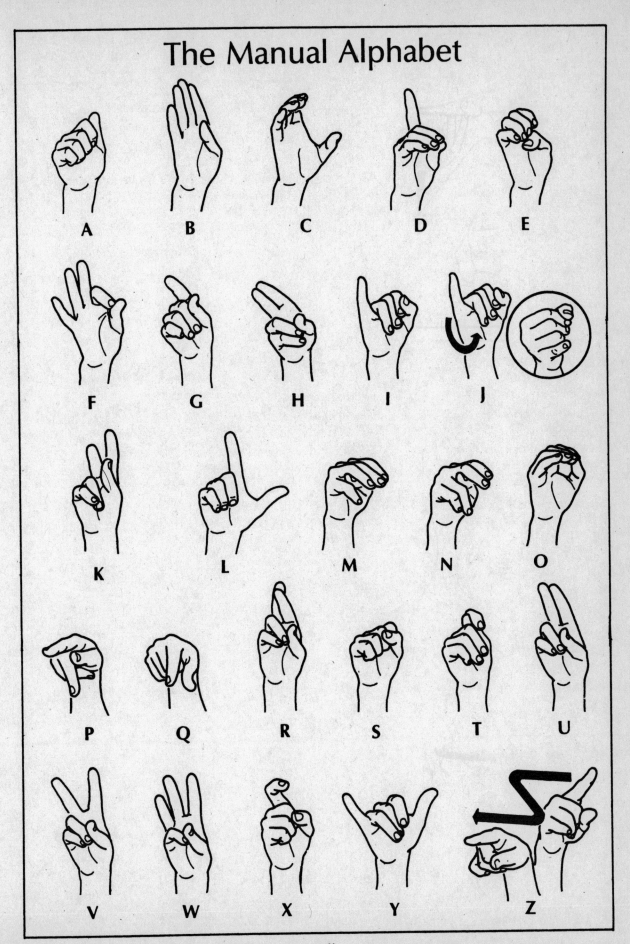

RELIGIOUS SIGNING

ABOVE, OVER

The hand moves to a position above the other hand and symbolizes the area on high from where God rules the world.

Formation: Starting with the downturned right open hand lying on the back of the downturned left open hand, elbows out, bring the right hand upward in a spiraling movement.

ABRAHAM

The formation of this sign represents God staying Abraham's arm as he raised the knife to slay his son, Isaac.

Formation: The right "a" hand, palm facing left, is brought down and forward from in front of the right shoulder deliberately. The cupped left hand, palm up, moves upward, clasping the right forearm and stopping it abruptly as it descends.

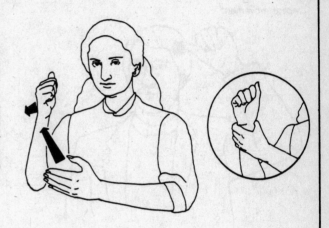

ABUNDANT, ABUNDANCE, PLENTY, PLENTIFUL, BOUNTIFUL

The hands indicate a cup that is full and overflowing.

Formation: Push the palm of the downturned open hand, fingers pointing forward, across the thumb side of the left "s" hand, palm right, curving downward over the left knuckles.

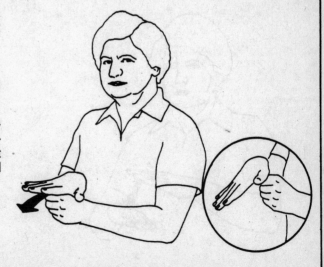

repeat movement

ACCUSE, BLAME, AT FAULT

This is a directional sign that seems to push responsibility or blame at whomever it is directed.

Formation: Move the right "a" hand, palm left and thumb extended upward, in a downward arc across the back of the downturned open left hand toward the referent.

Note: If you are being accused, direct the right thumb toward yourself. The left hand may be an "s" hand.

See also OBLIGATION for a sign with a related meaning.

repeat movement

ADAM

This is an initialized sign in the masculine position and signifies Adam's position as the first man.

Formation: Touch the right temple with the thumb of the right "a" hand, palm facing forward.

ADMONISH, ADMONITION, WARN

The sign represents a slap on the wrist as a warning.

Formation: Slap the back of the downturned left open hand with the fingers of the downturned right open hand with a double movement.

Same sign for CAUTION

ADULTERY (A)

The hand movement indicates the alternating attention that an unfaithful married person gives his or her spouse and then to another partner outside the marriage.

Formation: Tap the knuckles of the right "a" hand, palm facing outward, alternatively on each fingertip of the left "v" hand, palm facing the chest and the fingers pointing up.

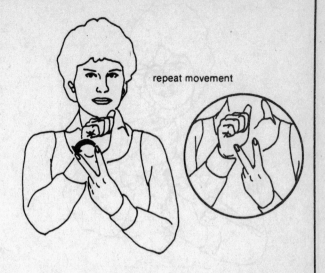

repeat movement

ADULTERY (B)

The sign seems to show someone slipping around the corner or behind someone's back for an affair.

Formation: Move the palm side of the right open hand, palm facing right and fingers pointing forward, across the palm of the left open hand, palm right and fingers pointing up, around the little-finger side.

ADVENT, COMING

This is a directional form of COME and signifies the birth of Christ and the preparation period of four weeks before Christmas.

Formation: Beginning with both extended index fingers pointing up, hands in front of and higher than the head, palms facing in, bring both hands down simultaneously while turning the palms down, ending with both index fingers pointing down in front of the chest.

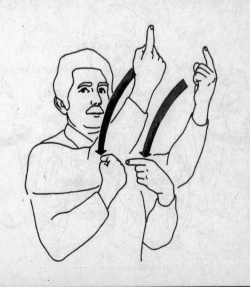

ADVOCATE, SUPPORT, FOUNDATION

The action of the left hand pushing the right hand upward shows active support for a cause.

Formation: Bring the knuckle side of the right "s" hand, palm facing the body, upward under the left "s" hand, palm facing the body, pushing it upward in front of chest.

Same sign for ADVOCACY, IN FAVOR OF

See also HELP for a sign formed in a similar manner.

AISLE, WAY

The hands outline a passageway, such as between rows of seats in a church.

Formation: Move both open hands forward simultaneously, palms facing each other and fingers pointing forward and held several inches apart in front of the waist.

Same sign for PATH, ROAD

repeat movement

ALLELUIA, HALLELUJAH

As an expression of praise of thanksgiving to God, this sign is a combination of PRAISE and CELEBRATION.

Formation: Bring both open hands, palms facing each other and fingertips pointing up, together in front of the chest. Then raise both modified "a" hands near each shoulder, moving them in small circles outward.

ALMIGHTY, OMNIPOTENT

This sign is a combination of ALL and POWER, an attribute referring to God's unlimited or universal power.

Formation: With the open right hand palm facing out, near the left shoulder, make a large loop to the right ending, palm up, in the upturned left palm. Then move the "s" hands, palms facing body, from the center of the chest outward with force, ending abruptly.

See also POWER AND MIGHTY for alternate signs.

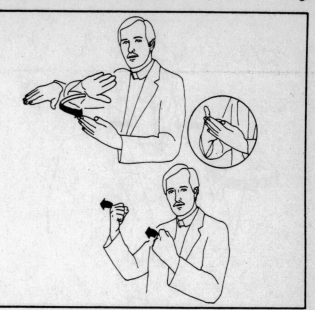

ALONE

The single finger moving in a circle is an emphatic form of the sign ONE.

Formation: With the right extended index finger pointing up, palm toward the body, rotate the arm and hand in a counter-clockwise circle.

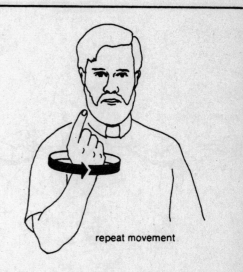

repeat movement

ALTAR

This sign is an initialized form of TABLE. The hands outline the shape of an altar, the structure before which the divine offices are recited and upon which the Eucharist is celebrated.

Formation: With the thumbs of both "a" hands touching each other in front of the chest, palms facing out, move the hands apart to about shoulder width and then downward a short distance without changing orientation.

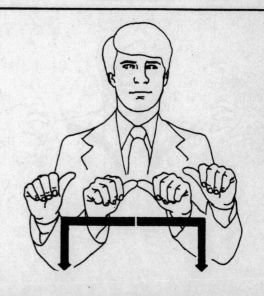

repeat movement

ALWAYS, EVER, CONSTANTLY

The circular motion of this sign shows something never ending.

Formation: Move the extended right index finger, palm angled upward, in a small circle clockwise near the right shoulder.

See also EVERLASTING for an alternate sign.

repeat movement

ANGEL, CHERUB, SERAPH

The hands represent the movement of wings traditionally attributed to angels, the immortal spiritual beings attending to God's will.

Formation: Touch the fingertips of both bent hands to the shoulders, palms facing down and elbows close at the sides. Turn the wrists outward and bend the hands up and down.

Same sign for WINGS

ANGER, WRATH, RAGE, FURY

The tense fingers represent angry emotions raised up in the body.

Formation: Bring both "claw" hands, knuckles pointed toward each other and palms toward the body, upward from near each other at the waist and out toward each shoulder.

ANNOUNCE, ANNOUNCEMENT, PROCLAIM, DECLARE, ANNUNCIATION, EVANGELISM

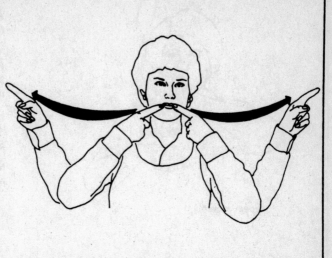

The fingers indicate taking words from the mouth and declaring them broadly.

Formation: Start with both extended index fingers touching each side of the mouth, palms facing in. Twist the wrists to bring the fingers outward past the shoulders, palms facing forward and fingers pointing at an angle upward.

Note: The distance the hands move outward indicates the size or importance of the announcement.

See also ANNUNCIATION and EVANGELISM (A) (B) for alternate signs.

ANNUNCIATION

This sign is a combination of ANNOUNCE and MARY and refers to the angel's announcement to the Virgin Mary that she would bear a son, Jesus.

Formation: Beginning with both extended index fingers touching each side of the mouth, palms facing in, twist the wrists and bring the fingers outward past the shoulders, palms facing forward and fingers pointing at an angle upward. Then bring the right "m" hand, palm toward the head, in an arc following the shape of the head, from the top of the left side of the head to the right shoulder.

ANOINT, LENT (A)

The sign symbolizes how a priest anoints a person's forehead with oil as a sign of consecration in a religious ceremony.

Formation: Draw the thumbnail of the right "a" hand, palm down, across the forehead first downward a short distance and then from left to right.

See also LENT for an alternate sign.

repeat movement

ANOINT, ATONE, ATONEMENT, OIL (B)

The hand seems to pour oil over another such as is done as a sign of consecration in a religious ceremony.

Formation: Move the thumb of the right "a" hand, pointing down, over the top of the left downturned "a" hand.

Note: The left hand may be an "s" hand instead.

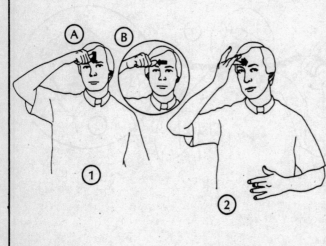

ANOINTING THE SICK

This sign is a combination of ANOINT and SICK. It is used in the Roman Catholic Church to indicate the sacrament, formerly known as Last Rites, administered by priests to terminally ill people.

Formation: Draw the thumbnail of the right "a" hand, palm down, across the forehead first downward a short distance and then from left to right. Then touch the bent middle finger of the right "5" hand to the forehead simultaneously while touching the bent middle finger of the left "5" hand to the stomach, both palms facing in.

ANSWER, RESPOND, RESPONSE, REPLY

The sign shows words directed from the mouth in reply.

Formation: Begin with the right extended index finger, palm left, in front of the lips and the left extended index finger, palm right, somewhat lower and forward. Bring both fingers downward simultaneously by bending the wrists forward.

Note: RESPONSE and REPLY are often initialized.

See also COMMAND (A) for a related sign formed in a similar manner.

APOSTOLIC

This sign is a combination of SINCE and FOLLOW and indicates that following that pertains to the faith, teaching, or practice of the apostles.

Formation: Touch both extended index fingertips just below the right shoulder. Move the fingers forward away from the body, ending with the fingers pointing forward and palms up. Then with the right "a" following the left "a" hand, palms facing toward each other, move both hands forward simultaneously in front of the body.

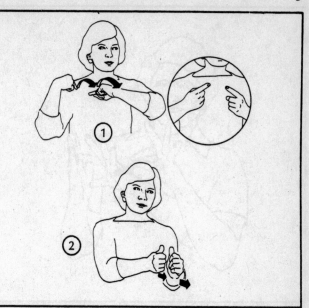

APPEAR, APPEARANCE

The right index finger popping up through the left hand indicates a sudden coming into view.

Formation: Push the right extended index finger, palm forward, upward deliberately between the index and middle fingers of the left hand held flat in front of the chest, palm down.

Same sign for SHOW UP, POP UP

See also: PRESENCE for the sign to use if referring to an appearance that is less sudden.

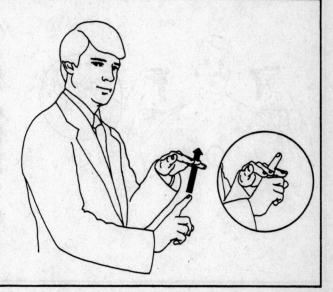

APPOINT, SELECT, CHOSEN, ELECT (A)

The fingers seem to select one out of available options.

Formation: Bring the bent thumb and index finger of the outstretched right "5" hand, back toward the right shoulder, closing the thumb to the index fingertip together.

Same sign for PICK, CHOOSE

APPOINT, SELECT, CHOSEN, ELECT (B)

The fingers seem to pick one out of many.

Formation: Bring the bent thumb and index finger of the right "5" hand from touching the left "5" palm, palms facing each other, back toward the right shoulder, closing the thumb to the index fingertip together.

Same Sign For PICK, CHOOSE

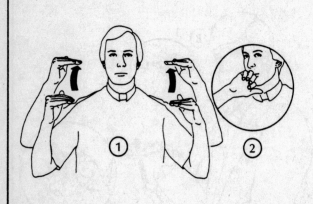

ARCHBISHOP

This sign is a combination of HIGH and BISHOP and indicates the highest ranking bishop who heads an archdiocese.

Formation: With both hands bent at right angles, palms facing each other and held near each shoulder, move them upward simultaneously, stopping abruptly at about eye level. Then with the palm facing outward, press the base of the ring finger of the loosely closed right hand to the lips.

ARCHDIOCESE

This sign is a combination of HIGH and DIOCESE and indicates the district under the jurisdiction of a archbishop.

Formation: With both hands at right angles, palms facing each other and held near each shoulder, move them upward simultaneously stopping abruptly at about eye level. Then with the fingertips of both "d" hands touching each other, palms facing, move the hands around in a small circle, until the little fingers touch and the palms face the body.

ASCENSION, ASCEND

The fingers represent a person standing on the ground and then ascending, as in the ascension of Christ into heaven, which is celebrated on the fortieth day after Easter.

Formation: Starting with the fingertips of the inverted "v" right hand in the up-turned flat left palm, pull the right hand straight upward.

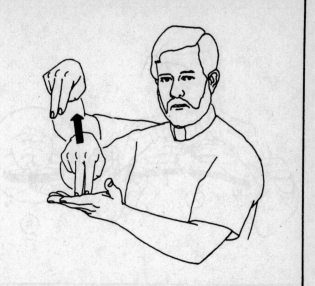

ASH WEDNESDAY

The sign is a combination of ANOINT and WEDNESDAY and indicates the custom of placing ashes on the forehead as a token of penitence on the first day of Lent, the seventh Wednesday before Easter.

Formation: Draw the thumbnail of the right "a" hand across the forehead first downward a short distance and then from left to right. Then move the right "w" hand, palm facing the chest, in a small circle.

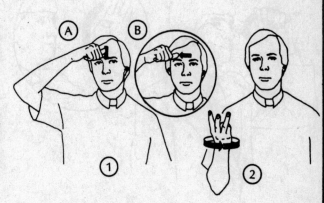

ASK, PETITION, REQUEST

This sign is a natural gesture used when requesting something. It is only used in the verb form.

Formation: Beginning with both open hands apart in front of the waist, palms facing each other and fingers pointing out, bring them back up toward the chest, closing the palms together as they move, and ending with the thumb side of both hands together touching the chest and the fingertips pointing upward.

Same sign for INQUIRE

See also PRAY for the noun form of this sign and BEG for a sign with a related meaning.

ASSEMBLE, GATHER, CONGREGATE

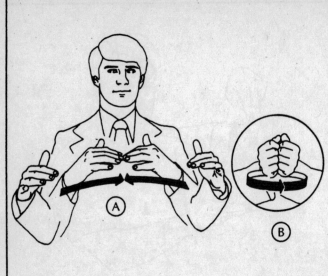

In the first part of the sign the fingers represent people flocking to a central location, such as a church or synagogue. The second part of the sign is the sign for TOGETHER.

Formation: Bring both loose "5" hands, palms down, from outside each side of the chest toward each other until the fingertips touch. Change to both "a" hands, palms facing each other and knuckles touching, and move them in a circular motion in front of the lower chest.

See also MEETING for the noun form of this sign.

ASSEMBLIES OF GOD

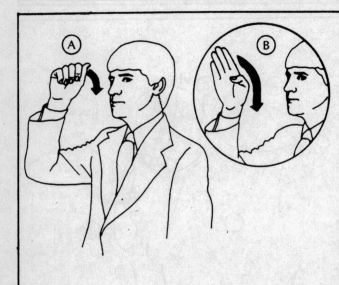

This sign, which is initialized and combined with GOD, refers to the largest of the Pentecostal sects, which was founded in 1914 and whose chief work is evangelistic and missionary.

Formation: Bring the thumb side of the right "a" hand to the forehead in a small downward arc. Then bring the right "b" hand, palm facing left and fingertips pointing up and slightly forward, in an arc toward the forehead and down in front of the face.

Note: The second part of the sign can be made with an open hand or a "g" hand instead of a "b" hand.

ASSUMPTION

The right hand represents the power of God taking the Virgin Mary, as represented by the left hand, bodily into heaven after her death.

Formation: Starting with the fingertips of the inverted "v" left hand in the upturned flat right palm, push the left hand upward by raising the right hand in front of the chest.

ASTONISH, ASTONISHMENT, AMAZE, AMAZEMENT

The sign depicts the eyes opening wide in great surprise.

Formation: With the extended thumb and index fingers of each hand pinched together at the outside corner of either eye, palms facing each other, flick the thumbs and index fingers apart simultaneously ending with the index finger pointing up and the thumb pointing toward either check.

Same sign for SURPRISE, SURPRISED

ATONE, ATONEMENT, VICARIOUS

This sign indicates one thing changing places with another and symbolizes Jesus's role taking man's punishment for sin upon himself in order to reconcile God and mankind.

Formation: With both "f" hands apart in front of body, palms facing each other and the right hand somewhat farther from the body than the left, circle the right hand up over the left toward the body while moving the left hand down and out to exchange positions with each other.

See also COVENANT and RECONCILE for related signs.

ATTEND, ATTENDANCE

This is the sign for GO TO formed with a double motion to indicate regularity.

Formation: With both "d" hands, palms facing outward and the right hand held somewhat closer to the body than the left hand, direct both extended index fingers outward and downward in a deliberate double motion.

repeat movement

BACKSLIDE, APOSTASY, STRAY, ASTRAY

The sign represents someone or something falling back, as when a person reverts from former religious practices to sinful ones.

Formation: Begin with both "a" hands, palms facing each other and knuckles touching. Pull right hand back toward the body in a wavy motion.

Same sign for BACK, BEHIND

See also STRAY for an alternate sign.

BAD, EVIL, WICKED

The hand seems to take something distasteful from the mouth and throw it away.

Formation: Starting with the fingertips of the right open hand on the lips, palm facing in, turn the wrist and move the hand down and outward from the mouth.

See also EVIL AND WICKED for alternate signs.

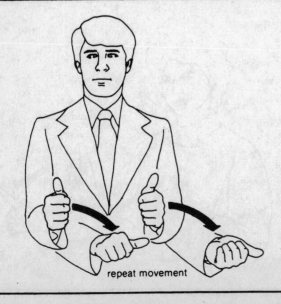

repeat movement

BAPTIZE, BAPTISM, IMMERSION, BAPTIST (A)

This sign indicates the dunking of a person's head under water. Since baptism by immersion is practiced by members of the Baptist Church, this sign is also used for BAPTIST.

Formation: Starting with both "a" hands several inches apart in front of the body, palms facing each other, dip the hands to the left two times, ending with the left palm facing up and the right palm facing down.

BAPTISM, BAPTIZE, CHRISTEN (B)

This sign is a combination of WATER and a gesture that indicates pouring water over the head of the person being baptized.

Formation: Tap the index-finger side of the right "w" hand, palm left, on the chin. Then tip the right "c" hand, palm left, over the top of the right side of the head, ending with the palm facing up.

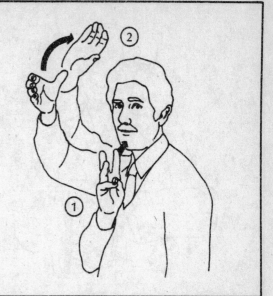

BAPTIZE, BAPTISM, CHRISTEN (C)

This sign is a combination of WATER and a gesture miming the sprinkling of water, which is used by some Christian churches during baptism, a sacrament in which the recipient is cleansed of Original Sin.

Formation: Tap the index-finger side of the right "w" hand, palm facing left, on the chin. Then holding the right hand above the right side of the head with the thumb and fingertips touching each other and pointing toward the head, flick the fingers open.

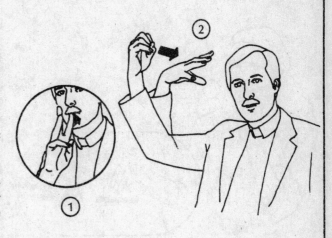

BAPTIZE, BAPTISM, CHRISTEN (D)

This sign is a combination of BABY and a gesture miming the sprinkling of water and signified the spiritual regeneration of an infant through baptism.

Formation: Place the fingertips of the open right hand, palm up, in the crook of the left elbow. The left arm rocking back and fourth. Then flick open the right "o" hand, palm down in front of the chest, over the bent left arm held in front of the body, palm up.

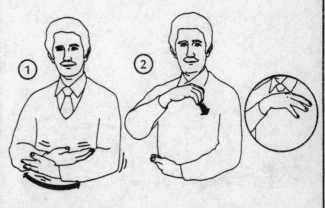

repeat movement

BAR MITZVAH, PHYLACTERIES, TEFIFFIN

The hand indicates the wrapping of a leather phylactery strap around the bare arm, a ritual taught to a Jewish boy preparing for his bar mitzvah, the ceremony following the successful completion of a course of Jewish studies. This ritual is performed by the man throughout his life.

Formation: Move the palm side of the right modified "a" hand around the left forearm extended across the body.

See also BAR MITZVAH and MITZVAH for related signs.

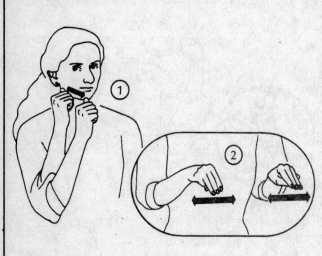

BAT MITZVAH

This sign is a combination of GIRL and MITZVAH and is used to refer to the ceremony that follows a Jewish girl's successful completion of a course of Jewish studies.

Formation: Drag the thumb of the right "a" hand, palm left, down the cheek along the jawline. Then move both "m" hands, palms down, back and forth in front of the waist.

See also BAR MITZVAH and MITZVAH for signs with related meanings.

BEG, ENTREAT, SUPPLICATION, PLEAD, INTERCEDE

This is the natural motion used by street beggars wanting coins.

Formation: Hold the extended left index finger under the wrist of the upturned right "claw" hand. Constrict the right fingers inward toward the palm in a repeated motion.

Note: The left hand may be a downturned "s" hand or may hold the right wrist instead.

See also ASK for a sign with a related meaning.

BEGINNING, INSTITUTED

The action of the hands indicates turning a key in the ignition to start a car.

Formation: Twist the right extended index finger, palm facing downward, between the index and middle fingers of the left "5" hand, palm facing right, until the right palm is facing upward.

Same sign for BEGIN, START, INITIATE

See also FOUNDED for a sign with a related meaning.

repeat movement

BEHOLD, WITNESS (A)

The extended fingers represent the gaze of the eyes.

Formation: Jab the fingers of both "v" hands forward in a double motion with the right hand a little closer to the chest than the left.

Same sign for LOOK, WATCH, OBSERVE

See also PROPHECY AND WITNESS (A) for signs with related meanings.

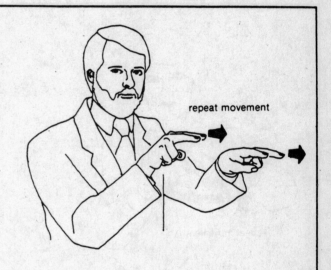

repeat movement

BEHOLD, WITNESS (B)

This sign is a combination of SEE and LOOK and signifies the practice of seeing something and observing it for a period of time.

Formation: Beginning with the fingertips of the right "v" hand, palm down, pointing at the eyes, twist the right wrist to point the fingers outward alongside the left "v" hand, fingers pointing forward and both palms facing down.

See also PROPHECY and WITNESS (A) for signs with related meanings.

BELIEVE, BELIEF, CONVICTION, CREED

This sign is a combination of THINK and a movement indicating taking a thought and holding it.

Formation: Move the extended right index finger smoothly down from the right temple, palm toward the face, to clasp the upturned left hand in front of the body, palms facing each other.

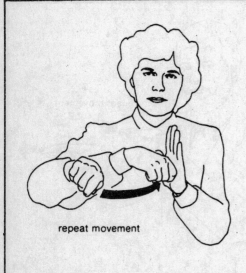

repeat movement

BELL (A)

The hand mimes the action of the clapper striking inside a bell.

Formation: Swing the right "a" hand, palm facing down, from right to left and strike the thumb side against the palm of the open left hand, palm right and fingers pointing up.

BELL (B)

The hand mimes the action of the clapper striking inside a bell.

Formation: Strike the thumb side of the right "a" hand, palm down, against the palm of the open left hand, palm right and fingers pointing up. Then bounce the right hand to the right with a wavy motion.

BELOVED, CHARITY, DEVOTION, REVERE, LOVE

The hands seem to clasp something near the heart and indicates someone or something held with great affection.

Formation: With both palms facing the body, hold the left flat hand across the right flat hand, which is held on the heart area of the chest.

See also LOVE for an alternate sign.

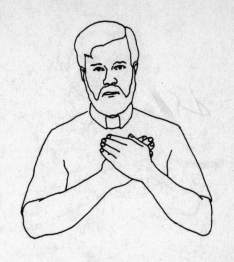

BELOW

The hands demonstrate that something is below another.

Formation: Starting with the downturned right open hand under the palm of the downturned left open hand, bring the right hand downward in a spiraling movement.

BENEDICTION, MONSTRANCE

The hands hold an imaginary monstrance, the receptacle containing the Host in the Roman Catholic Church, and move it in the shape of a cross.

Formation: With the right "s" hand held on top of the thumb side of the left "s" hand, palms facing each other, move both hands from in front of the face down in front of the chest. Then, keeping the hands in the same position, move them across in front of the face from left to right.

See also BLESSING for another sign for BENEDICTION used in other faiths.

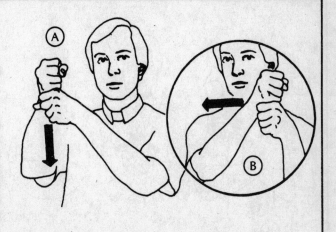

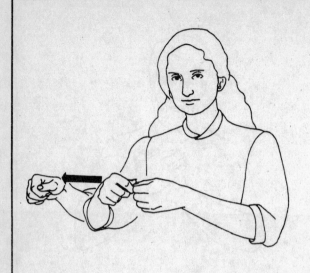

BENTSH LICHT

The hands mime the natural gesture of striking a match and refers to the kindling of the Sabbath lights.

Formation: Strike the thumbtip of the right "a" hand on the thumbnail of the left "a" hand, palms toward the chest, bringing the right hand forward with a flick of the wrist.

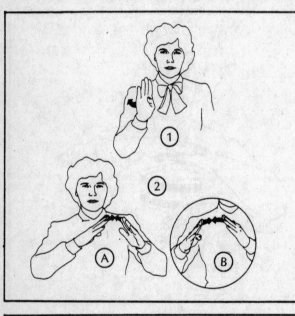

BETHLEHEM

This is a combination of an initialized sign and TOWN and refers to the town in Israel where David lived and Jesus was born.

Formation: Move the right "b" hand, palm facing outward, slightly upward near the right shoulder. Then with palms facing and hands held at an angle, tap the fingertips together first in front of the left chest and then again in front of the right chest.

See also JERUSALEM (A) and NAZARETH for initialized signs formed in a similar manner.

BIBLE (A)

This sign is a combination of JESUS and BOOK and refers to the sacred book of Christianity including the books of both the Old Testament and the New Testament.

Formation: Touch the bent middle finger of the right "5" hand into the center of the left palm, palms facing each other. Reverse the action by touching the bent middle finger of the left "5" hand into the right palm. Then starting with both palms touching in front of the chest, fingers pointing forward, move the hands apart at the top, keeping the little fingers together.

BIBLE (B)

This sign is formed like BOOK and refers to God's word coming down from heaven.

Formation: Beginning with the palms of both open hands closed together above the head, fingertips pointing up, bring the hands downward to in front of the chest, ending with the palms of both open hands facing upward, keeping the fingers together.

BIBLE, HOLY SCRIPTURE, TANACH (C)

This sign is a combination of HOLY and BOOK and refers to the sacred book for those of the Jewish faith.

Formation: Form an "h" with the right hand above the upturned left palm. Move the "h" fingers across the upturned left palm from its base to off the fingertips, keeping the fingers perpendicular to each other. Then starting with both palms touching in front of the chest, fingers pointing forward, move the hands apart at the top, keeping the little fingers together.

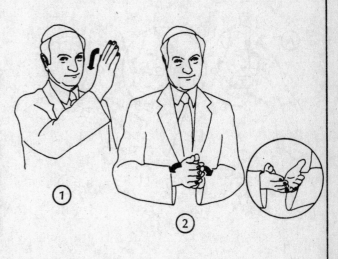

BIBLE, HOLY SCRIPTURE, TANACH (D)

This sign is a combination of GOD and BOOK and is used by members of the Jewish faith.

Formation: Move the right "b" hand, palm left, from above the front of the head, downward in an arc toward the forehead and down in front of the face. Then starting with both palms touching each other in front of the chest, fingers pointing forward, move the hands apart at the top, keeping the little fingers together.

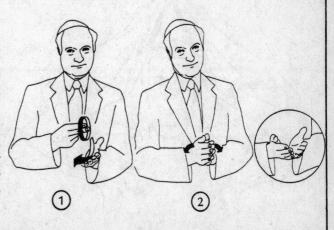

BIRTH, BORN, NATIVITY, CONCEPTION

The right hand seems to bring the baby forth from the womb and presents it for view.

Formation: Bring the right open palm from on the stomach outward, landing palm up on the upturned left palm.

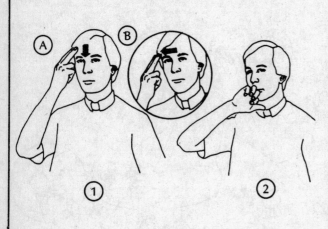

BISHOP (A)

This sign is a combination of CATHOLIC and a gesture symbolizing the custom of kissing the bishop's ring in the Roman Catholic Church.

Formation: Draw the right "u" hand downward in front of the forehand, palm toward the face and fingers pointing up. Then bring the "u" hand, fingers still pointing up, from left to right in front of the forehead. Then the palm facing outward, press the base of the ring finger of the loosely closed right hand to the lips.

BISHOP, MITER (B)

The hands follow the shape of the imaginary miter worn by a bishop, a high-ranking Christian clergyman.

Formation: With the palms of both flat hands held facing each side of the head, move them upward at an angle until the fingertips touch above the head.

See also POPE for a sign formed in a similar manner.

BLASPHEMY, CURSE, SWEAR (A)

The hands indicate taking words from the mouth and shoving them angrily at heaven as an act of dishonor for the being or work of God.

Formation: Beginning with the thumb of the right "c" hand, palm left, at the edge of the mouth, move the hand abruptly upward while closing to an "s" hand.

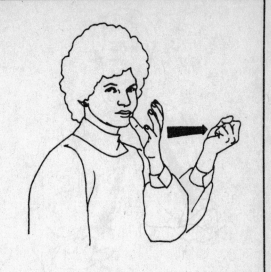

BLASPHEMY, CURSE, SWEAR (B)

The hands indicated taking words from the mouth and shoving them angrily at hell.

Formation: Beginning with the thumb of the right "c" hand, palm left, at the edge of the mouth, move the hand abruptly downward while closing into an "s" hand.

BLEED, SHED

This sign is a combination of RED and a movement of the hands that symbolizes blood trickling from an artery.

Formation: With the left "5" hand in front of the chest, palm toward the body and fingers pointing right, bring the right "5" hand, palm toward the body and fingers pointing left, from touching the lips down past the left hand. Move the right hand to the back of the left hand and repeat a couple of times.

See also BLOOD for the noun form.

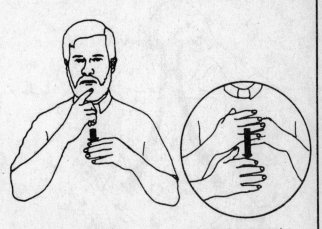

repeat movement

BLESS, BLESSING, ABSOLUTION, BENEDICTION (A)

The hands indicate taking a prayer from the mouth and directing it over the person or thing being blessed in a natural gesture.

Formation: Place the thumbnails of both "a" hands from near the mouth, palms facing each other. Move the hands downward and outward, opening into downturned "5" hands.

See also BENEDICTION for a related sign used by Roman Catholics.

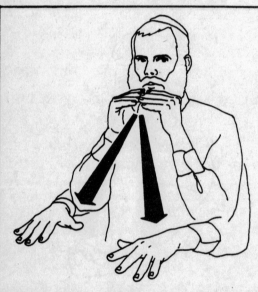

BLESS, BLESSING, ABSOLUTION, BENEDICTION (B)

The hands seem to take the words of blessing from the mouth and spread them over the person or thing being blessed.

Formation: Beginning with the fingertips of both bent hands touching each other in front of the mouth, palms facing down, move the hands downward and outward while opening to downturned "5" hands.

See also BENEDICTION for a form of this sign used by Roman Catholics.

BLESS, BLESSING (C)

The hands indicate taking a prayer from the mind and spreading it out to sanctify someone or something.

Formation: Place the thumbnails of both "a" hands on the forehead, palms facing each other. Move the hands downward and outward to in front of the waist, opening into downturned "5" hands as they move.

BLOOD

This sign is a combination of RED and a movement of the hands that symbolizes blood trickling from an artery.

Formation: With the left "5" hand in front of the chest palm toward body and fingers pointing right, bring the right "5" hand, palm toward body and fingers pointing left, from touching the lips down past the left hand, wiggling the fingers as the hand moves.

See also BLEED for the verb form.

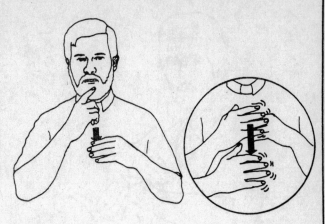

BOARD

This initialized sign is formed like MEMBER and refers to an organized, decision-making group.

Formation: Touch the thumb side of the right "b" hand, palm left, first near the left shoulder and then near the right shoulder.

See also BOARD OF DEACONS, DEACONS (B), and MEMBER for other initialized signs formed in a similar manner.

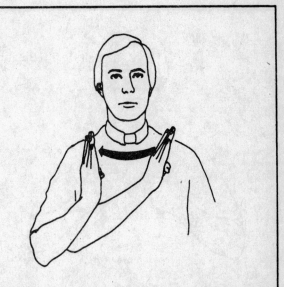

BOARD OF DEACONS

This initialized sign is formed like MEMBER and refers to an organized group of leaders in some denominations.

Formation: Touch the thumb side of the right "b" hand, palm left, near the left shoulder. Then while moving the hand across the chest, change it to a "d" hand, touching it near the right shoulder, palm toward body.

See also BOARD, DEACON (B), and MEMBER for other initialized signs formed in a similar manner.

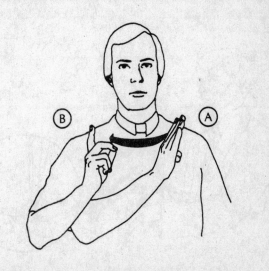

BREAD, HOST, MANNA

The hands mime cutting slices of bread from a loaf. The sign refers to the unleavened bread used in religious rites.

Formation: Roll the little-finger edge of the bent right hand down over the back of the left bent hand, palm facing the body, several times.

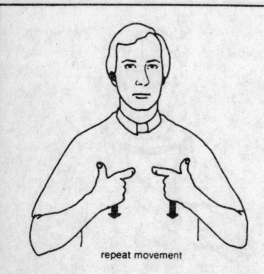

repeat movement

BROTHER, CHRISTIAN BROTHER

The fingers follow the shape of the stole worn by the clergy.

Formation: Move the thumb and index fingertips of both hands, palms facing body, downward simultaneously on the chest a short distance.

See also TALLITH for a Jewish sign formed in a similar manner.

BURY, GRAVE

The hands indicate the mound of dirt that covers a grave.

Formation: Move both curved down-turned open hands, fingers pointing forward, back toward the body in an arc.

Note: The hands may begin as "a" hands and open as they move back toward the body.

CALL, CALLED, VOCATION (A)

This is a directional variation of the sign normally used for CALL or SUMMON. The direction of the movement indicates a calling from God, representing the predisposition or desire to undertake a religious career.

Formation: Slap the back of the downturned open left hand from the outside with the fingers of the downturned right hand, fingers pointing toward chest. Pull the right hand back away quickly while bending fingers into palm.

See also VOCATION (A) (B) for alternate signs.

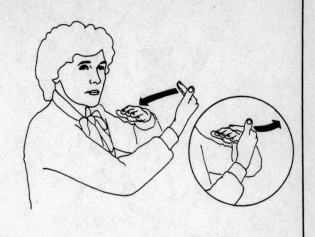

CALL, CALLED, INVITE, INVITATION (B)

The hand makes a natural welcoming motion to bring another in close to oneself, similar to God's invitation to mankind to become his children.

Formation: Swing the upturned curved right hand from in front of the body inward toward the waist in an arc.

CALVARY

This sign is a combination of MOUNTAIN and CROSS and represents the hill outside ancient Jerusalem where Jesus was crucified.

Formation: Tap the knuckles of the right "s" hand on the back of the downturned left "s" hand. Move both open hands, angled forward, upward to the left with a wavy movement, left hand higher than the right. Move the right "c" hand, palm facing outward, first down from above the right side of the head to the right side of the body, then from left to right in front of the right shoulder.

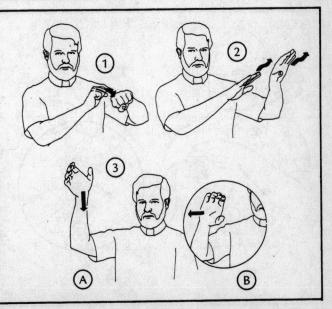

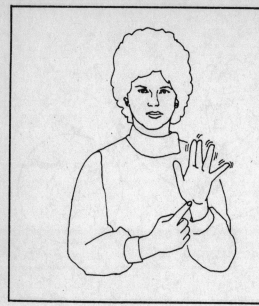

CANDLE

The wiggling fingers indicate the motion of flickering candlelight.

Formation: While holding the right extended index finger, palm facing in, at the wrist of the left "5" hand, palm facing out, wiggle the left fingers.

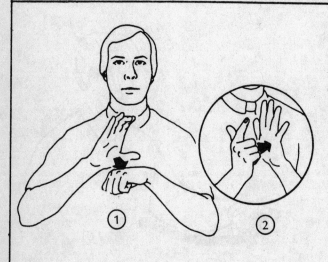

CANON LAW

This sign is a combination of CHURCH and LAW and represents the ecclesiastical code of laws established by a church council.

Formation: Tap the thumb side of the right "c" hand on the back of the left "s" hand, palm down. Then strike the right "l" on the left open palm, palms facing each other.

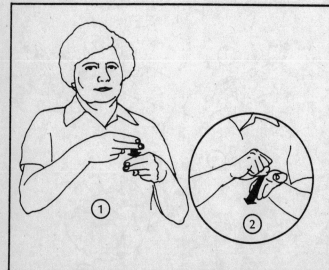

CANONIZE

This sign is a combination of NAME and SAINT and refers to the practice in the Roman Catholic Church of declaring a deceased person to be a saint and entitled to be fully honored as such.

Formation: Tap the middle-finger side of the right "h" fingers on the index-finger side of the left "h" fingers held perpendicular to each other. Then drag the palm side of the right "s" hand across the upturned left palm from its base to the fingertips and outward.

CANTOR

This is a combination of an initialized sign formed like SONG and the person marker and designates the chief singer of the liturgy in a synagogue.

Formation: Swing the right "c" hand, palm left, back and forth in a large arc over the extended upturned left arm. Add the person marker.

See also CHOIR (A), HYMN, and PSALM for other signs formed in a similar manner.

CARDINAL (A)

This sign, a combination of RED and BISHOP, indicates the highest-ranking position in the Roman Catholic Church and refers to the vivid red cassock worn by cardinals, who are appointed by the Pope.

Formation: Stroke downward on the lips with the extended right index finger, palm toward face. Then with the palm facing outward, press the base of the ring finger of the loosely closed right hand to the lips.

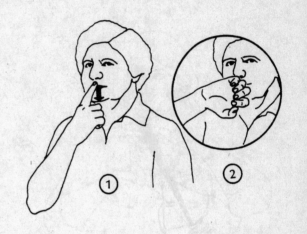

CARDINAL (B)

This is an old sign still used in certain cities, such as Baltimore, New York City, and Buffalo.

Formation: Tap the inside edge of the right "i" finger, palm left, against the middle of the chin in a short double motion.

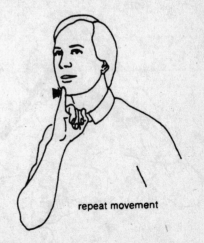

repeat movement

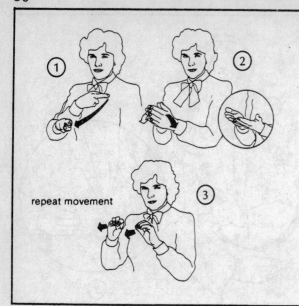

CATECHISM

This sign is a combination of RELIGION, BOOK, and TEACH and indicates the book that presents a brief summary, in question and answer form, of the basic principles or beliefs of any given religion.

Formation: Bring the fingertips of the right "r" hand from the left side of the chest, palm facing in, down and outward, ending with the palm facing down and the fingers pointing forward. Then starting with both palms together and fingers pointing forward, move the hands apart at the top, keeping the little fingers together. Finally with the thumbs touching the fingertips of both hands, palms facing forward, move the hands forward in front of the chest with a short double motion.

repeat movement

CATHEDRAL (A)

This initialized sign is formed like CHURCH with a gesture that indicates that it is higher, signifying a large or important church.

Formation: Move the right "c" hand, palm facing forward, from on the back of the downturned left "s" hand upward in an arc to the right.

See also SYNAGOGUE for an initialized sign formed in a similar manner.

CATHEDRAL (B)

This initialized sign follows the shape of a cathedral's dome.

Formation: Move the right "c" hand, palm left, from near the left shoulder to near the top of the head to near the right shoulder.

CATHOLIC, ROMAN CATHOLIC

This is the traditional sign of the cross made on the forehead, representing the Christian church that is characterized by leadership by apostolic succession with the Pope as its head.

Formation: Draw the right "u" hand downward in front of the forehead, palm toward the face and the fingers pointing up. Then bring the "u" hand, fingers still pointing up, from left to right in front of the forehead.

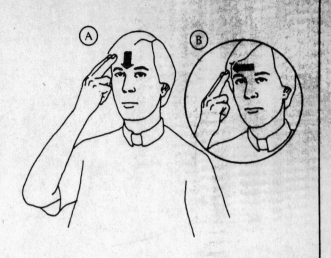

CELIBACY

This initialized sign is formed like BACHE-LOR and signified the practice among Roman Catholic clergy to never marry.

Formation: Move the right "c" hand, palm left, downward a short distance first at the left side of the chin and then again at the right side of the chin.

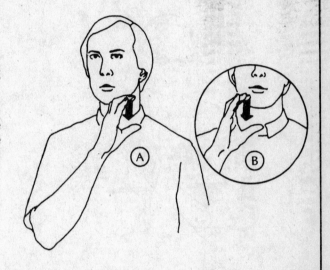

CELEBRATE, CELEBRATION, REJOICE, TRIUMPH, FESTIVAL, VICTORY

The hands seem to be waving small flags in celebration.

Formation: Make small circles above both shoulders with both modified "a" hands, palms facing each other and index finger knuckles extended.

Note: This sign may be formed with only one hand.

See also VICTORY for a sign formed in a similar manner.

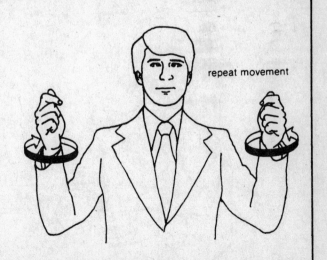

repeat movement

CHALICE, CUP, GLASS

The right hand follows the shape of a chalice, the cup used for the consecrated wine of the Eucharist.

Formation: Move the right "c" hand, palm left, upward a few inches from the up-turned left palm.

CHANUKAH, HANUKKAH, FESTIVAL OF LIGHTS

The hands form the shape of a menorah, a nine-branched candelabrum used during this holiday, which commemorates the victory of the Maccabees over the Syrians in 165 B.C. and the rededication of the temple in Jerusalem.

Formation: Begin with both "4" hands in front of the center of the chest, palms facing in. Then move the hands outward, away from each other, while spreading the fingers apart slightly.

CHAPTER

This initialized sign seems to outline a column of words in a passage of text, such as in the Scriptures.

Formation: With the left open hand held in front of body, palm facing right and fingertips pointing forward, move the fingertips of the right "c" hand downward across the left palm.

CHARISMATIC (A)

This initialized sign indicates speaking in tongues, the basis of the charismatic belief.

Formation: Beginning with the thumb of the right "c" hand near the mouth, palm left, move it outward in small double arcs.

CHARISMATIC (B)

This initialized sign is formed like PENTECOST, the festival sometimes known as the start of speaking in tongues, which is part of the charismatic belief.

Formation: Tap the right "c" hand, palm facing outward, downward once in front of the body and again slightly to the right.

See also PENTECOST and TONGUE for other signs with related meanings.

CHOIR (A)

This is an initialized form of MUSIC. The movement shows the rhythmic sway of music.

Formation: Swing the palm side of the right "c" hand back and forth in an arc over the extended left forearm.

See also CANTOR, HYMN, and PSALM for other signs formed in a similar manner.

repeat movement

CHOIR (B)

This sign is a combination of SONG and GROUP and designates an organized company of church singers.

Formation: Swing the right open hand back and forth in a large arc of the extended left forearm, fingers forward and palm right. Then move both "c" hands, palms facing each other in front of the chest, in a circle outward until the little fingers meet.

CHRIST

This is an initialized sign following the sash worn by royalty. The sign signified the Messiah, as foretold by the prophets of the Old Testament.

Formation: Touch the index-finger side of the right "c" hand, palm left, first to the left shoulder and then to the right hip.

See also DAVID, KING, LORD (A), and MESSIAH for other initialized signs formed in a similar manner.

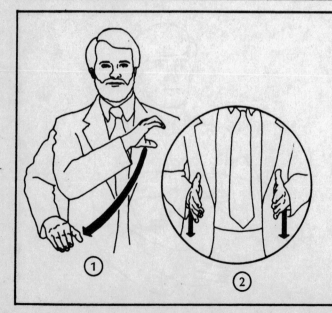

CHRISTIAN (A)

The sign is a combination of CHRIST and the person marker and refers to persons following the religion based on Jesus Christ's teachings.

Formation: Touch the index-finger side of the "c" hand, palm left, first to the left shoulder and then to the right hip. Add the person marker.

CHRISTIAN (B)

This sign is a combination of JESUS and the person marker and signifies the followers of Jesus Christ and his teachings.

Formation: Touch the bent middle finger of the right "5" hand into the center of the left palm, palms facing each other. Reverse the action by touching the bent middle finger of the left "5" hand into the right palm. Add the person marker.

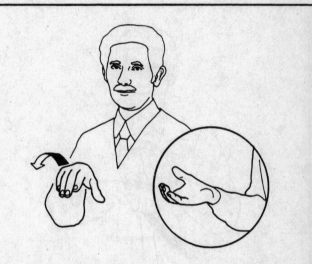

CHRISTMAS (A)

The hand of this initialized sign mimes opening a present and designates the holiday on December 25 celebrating the birth of Jesus.

Formation: Flip the right "c" hand, palm down and knuckles forward, to the right, ending with the palm facing up.

Note: The sign may be made with two "c" hands.

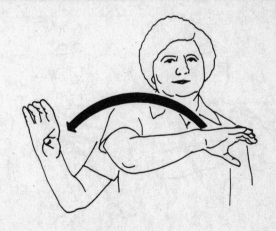

CHRISTMAS (B)

The hand of this initialized sign follows the shape of a wreath.

Formation: Move the right "c" hand from near the left shoulder, palm down, in a large arc ending near the right shoulder, palm facing outward.

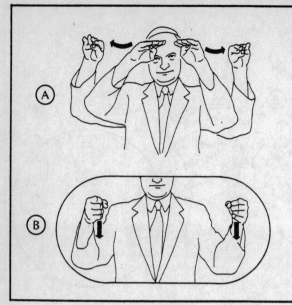

CHUPPAH

The hands outline the shape of a chuppah, the wedding tent used in Jewish weddings.

Formation: Bring both downturned "b" hands from near each other in front of the forehead, outward beyond each shoulder in a slight arc. Then change to both "s" hands bringing them from above each shoulder straight downward, palms facing each other.

See also SUKKOTH for another sign formed in a similar manner.

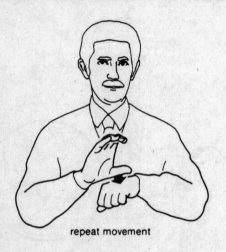

repeat movement

CHURCH, DENOMINATION, CHAPEL, ECCLESIASTICAL

This is an initialized sign symbolizing the rock of faith, the left hand, upon which the church was founded as described in the New Testament.

Formation: Tap the thumb side of the right "c" hand on the back of the left "s" hand, palm facing down.

See also PETER, LUTHERAN (B), PARISH, and TEMPLE for other initialized signs formed in a similar manner.

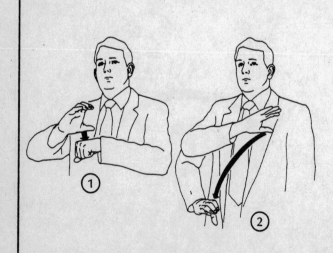

CHURCH OF CHRIST (A)

The sign is a combination of CHURCH and CHRIST.

Formation: Tap the thumb side of the right "c" hand on the back of the left "s" hand, palm facing down. Then touch the index-finger side of the right "c" hand, palm left, first to the left shoulder and then to the right hip.

CHURCH OF CHRIST (B)

This is an initialized sign.

Formation: Tap the right "c" hand, palm left, in the air in front of the center of the chest and then in front of the right side of the chest.

CHURCH OF GOD

This sign is a combination of CHURCH and GOD.

Formation: Tap the thumb side of the right "c" hand on the back of the left "s" hand, palm facing down. Then bring the right "b" hand, palm facing left and fingertips pointing up and slightly forward, in an arc toward the forehead and down in front of the face.

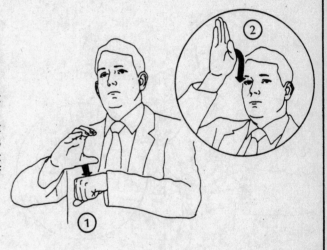

CIRCUMCISION (A)

The fingers mime the removal of the male prepuce and refers to the religious ceremony in which a person is circumcised and thereby spiritually purified.

Formation: Move the extended thumb of the right "a" hand in a circle around the extended thumb of the left "a" hand, both palms facing down.

CIRCUMCISION (B)

This sign mimes the act of circumcision, which, when performed as a religious rite, cleanses the participants from sin.

Formation: Move the extended thumb of the right "a" hand, palm down, in a circle around the extended left index finger, palm toward the body.

CIRCUMCISION, BRIS MILAH (C)

The hand mimes cutting away the male prepuce with scissors, a religious rite performed on a male child on the eighth day after his birth.

Formation: Close the fingers of the right "v" hand, palm facing left and fingers pointing forward, at the tip of the left extended index finger, palm facing down.

repeat movement

CLEANSE, WASH

The motion of this sign indicates scrubbing something until it is clean. In a religious sense it means to free from defilement of guilt.

Formation: Rub the right "a" knuckles, palm down, back and forth on the knuckles of the upturned left "a" hand.

COLLECTION, OFFERING

This sign is a combination of GATHER and MONEY and indicates the process of collecting money during a church service as an offering to God.

Formation: Beginning with the cupped right hand near the right side of the body, sweep it to the left, dragging the little-finger side from the fingers to the heel across the upturned left hand, closing the hand to an "s" handshape. Then tap the back of the fingers of the right hand, fingertips touching the thumb and palm facing up, in the palm of the upturned left hand in a double motion.

See also OFFERING for an alternate sign.

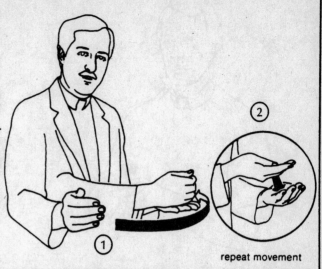

repeat movement

COMFORT, COMFORTABLE, SOOTHE

This sign demonstrates stroking the hands in a smooth, comforting manner.

Formation: Bring the palm of the downturned curved right hand down over the fingers of the downturned curved left hand. Repeat with the left over the right.

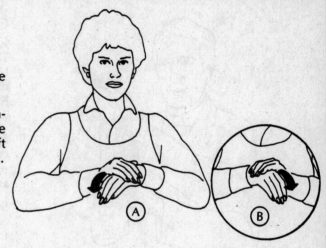

COMMAND, ORDER (A)

The hand indicates words being directed deliberately from the mouth.

Formation: Bring the extended right index finger, palm left, forward and downward from pointing at the mouth in a deliberate movement, ending with the finger pointing forward, palm facing down.

Note: This sign may be formed with two hands.

See also ANSWER for a related sign formed in a similar manner.

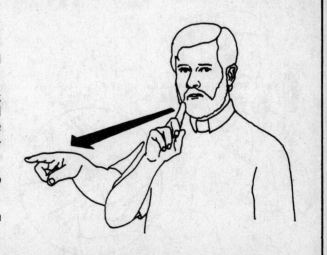

COMMAND, DEMAND, REQUIRE (B)

The finger seems to hook into something that it requires and brings it to the body and refers to God's commandments to mankind.

Formation: Strike the fingertip of the right "x" hand, palm left, against the open left palm, facing right. Bring both hands toward the chest.

COMMANDMENTS

This is an initialized sign formed like LAW. The Ten Commandments constitute the laws of God given to man; the left hand may symbolize the stone tablet on which the commandments were written.

Formation: Move the index-finger side of the right "c" hand, palm facing fingers pointing up, touching first the fingertips and then the heel of the left hand.

See also HALACHA (B), LAW (B), MOSES, and TESTAMENT for other initialized signs formed in a similar manner.

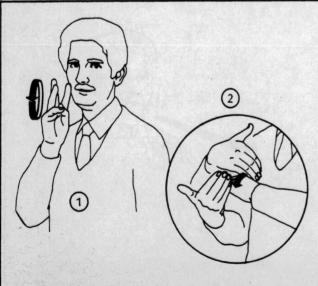

COMMUNION, HOLY COMMUNION, EUCHARIST (A)

This sign is a combination of WINE and BREAD, the consecrated elements used in this sacrament.

Formation: Stroke the index-finger side of the right "w" hand in small circles on the right cheek. Then with the left bent open hand facing the body, roll the little-finger edge right bent hand down over the back of the left hand several times.

COMMUNION, HOLY
COMMUNION, EUCHARIST,
HOST (B)

The fingertips move an imaginary Host in the shape of a cross in front of the lips.

Formation: With the right "f" hand, palm toward face, move the fingertips of the closed thumb and index finger first down and then from left to right in front of the lips.

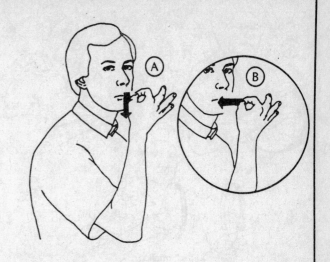

COMMUNION,
LORD'S SUPPER (C)

This sign is a combination of LORD and EAT and signifies the Last Supper eaten by Christ with his disciples on the night before his Crucifixion.

Formation: Touch the thumb of the right "l" hand, palm left and index finger point outward at an angle, first to the left shoulder and then to the right hip. Then with the right thumb and fingertips together, palm facing down, repeatedly move the fingertips toward the lips with short movements.

COMMUNION OF SAINTS (A)

This sign is a combination of UNITY and SAINTS and indicates the common religious faith that unites Christians.

Formation: With the thumbtip and index fingertip of each hand touching and intersecting with the other hand, palms facing each other, move the hands in a flat circle in front of the body. Then drag the palm side of the right "s" hand across the upturned left palm from its base to the fingertips and outward.

See also UNITY for an alternate sign.

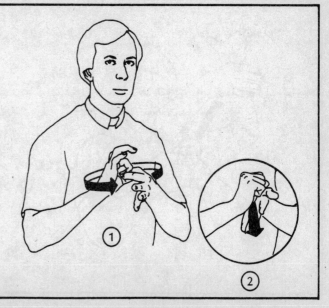

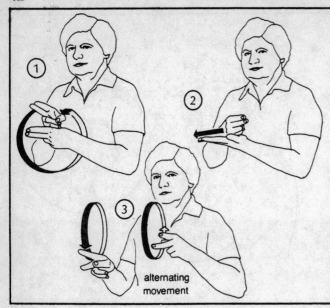

COMMUNION OF SAINTS (B)

This sign is a combination of UNIVERSAL, HOLY and PEOPLE and refers to the whole body of Christians, both living and dead, who are united through a common faith.

Formation: Bring the right "u" hand, palm left and fingers angles upward, in a circle over and around the left "u" hand, palm right and fingers angles upward. Then move the little-finger side of the right "h" hand across the upturned open left palm from its base to off the fingertips keeping the fingers perpendicular to each other. Finally, using both "p" hands, circle them outward with alternating movements.

alternating movement

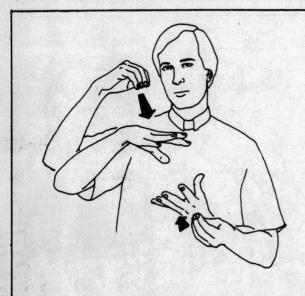

CONCEIVE (A)

The formation of this sign indicates Mary's conception occurring from the Holy Spirit.

Formation: Beginning with the thumb and fingertips of each hand pinched together, right hand held near the right side of the head, fingers pointing down, and left hand held in front of the chest, fingers pointing up, bring the hands toward each other opening the fingers into "5" hands, stopping apart in front of the face, palms facing each other.

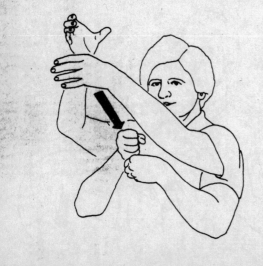

CONCEIVE (B)

This sign is a directional form of RECEIVE and refers to the Virgin Mary conceiving by the Holy Spirit.

Formation: With both "c" hands held above the head, palms facing each other and the right hand held higher than the left, bring them quickly down to the chest while closing to "s" hands, ending with the little-finger side of the right hand on top of the index-finger side of the left hand.

See also OBTAIN for a sign formed in a similar manner.

CONDEMN, JUDGMENT, ANNUL, ANNULMENT

The hand crosses out something as a declaration or judgment against it.

Formation: Using the extended right index finger, draw a large X across the upturned left palm.

Note: When referring to the Last Judgment, the movements should be large and deliberate.

Same sign for CANCEL, CORRECT, CRITICIZE, REVOKE

See also JUDGMENT for an alternate sign.

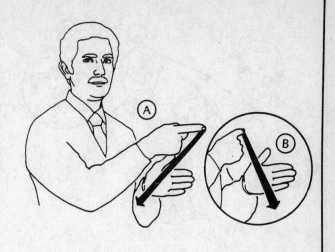

CONFESS, ADMIT, ACKNOWLEDGE

This sign indicates getting something off one's chest, as in the confession of sins.

Formation: Move both open hands from touching the chest, palms facing in and the fingers pointing toward each other, outward by twisting the wrists, ending with both palms up.

See also CONFESSION for the noun form of this sign.

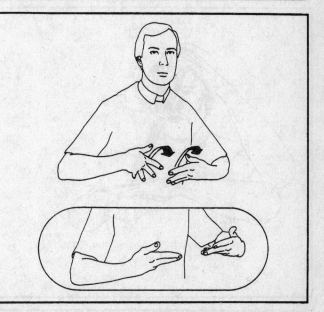

CONFESSION, PENANCE, CONFESSIONAL

This sign is a combination CONFESS and a gesture signifying the grating of a confessional stall through which a priest hears a person's confession of sins.

Formation: Move both open hands from touching the chest, palms facing in and fingers pointing toward each other, outward by twisting the wrists. Then place the back of the right "5" hand diagonally across the palm of the left "5" near the right side of the face.

See also CONFESS for the verb form of this sign.

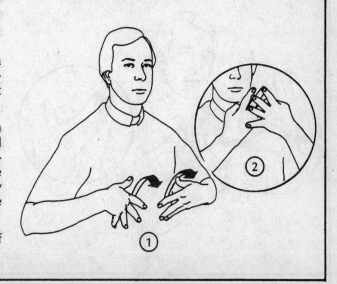

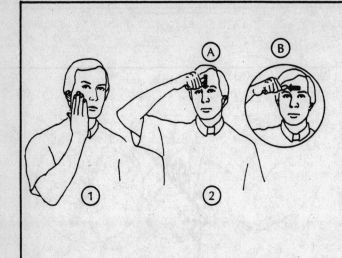

CONFIRMATION (A)

The sign indicates the Roman Catholic custom of slapping and then laying the hands on the hand of the confirmand being admitted to the church through this sacrament, which renews the vows of baptism.

Formation: Slap the open right palm against the right cheek. Then draw the thumbnail of the right "a" hand, palm down, across the forehead first downward a short distance and then from left to right.

See also INSTALL and ORDAIN for signs with related meanings.

CONFIRMATION (B)

This sign indicates blessing the imaginary head of the confirmand in front of the pastor or priest.

Formation: Bring the open right hand, palm down, from on top of the head to on the back of the left "s" hand, palm down.

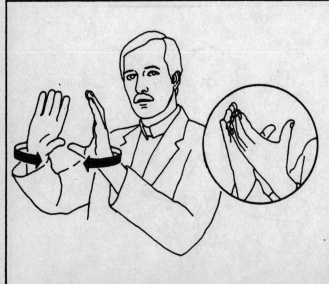

CONGREGATION, ASSOCIATION, ORGANIZATION, SYNOD, SOCIETY

The hands seem to encircle a group of people, such as members of specific religious groups who regularly worship at a common church.

Formation: Move both "c" hands, palms facing each other in front of the chest, in a circular movement outward.

Note: ORGANIZATION, SOCIETY, and ASSOCIATION are often formed with initialized handshapes.

See also DIOCESE, ERUV, and SOCIETY for other initialized signs with related meanings formed in a similar manner.

CONQUER, DEFEAT, OVERCOME, SUBDUE

This sign suggests forcing a person's head down in humbling defeat.

Formation: Move the right "s" hand, palm forward, forward and down with force over the downturned left "s" hand held in front of the chest ending with the right wrist resting on the back of the left hand and the hand hanging down.

Same sign for BEAT

CONSCIENCE, CONVICTION, GUILT, GUILTY (A)

The sign is a natural gesture for scolding directed at the heart, which traditionally governs a person's discrimination of right and wrong.

Formation: Tap the thumb side of the right hand with an extended index finger, palm down and finger pointing upward at an angle, on the upper left side of the chest several times.

repeat movement

CONSCIENCE, CONVICTION, GUILT, GUILTY (B)

This is an initialized sign formed near the heart and signifies feeling responsibility for some reprehensible act.

Formation: Tap the index-finger side of the right "g" hand, palm facing down, on the upper left side of the chest several times.

repeat movement

CONSECRATE, CONSECRATION

This sign is a combination of OFFER and HOLY and signifies the practice in some liturgical churches of changing the elements of Communion into the body and blood of Christ.

Formation: Raise both open hands, palms facing up, from in front of the waist upward. Then move the little-finger side of the right "h" hand across the upturned open left palm from its base to off the fingertips, keeping the fingers perpendicular to each other.

CONSERVATIVE

This is an initialized sign formed like CLEAN and signifies those Jews who accept some liturgical and ritual changes in traditional Jewish laws in light of the needs of modern life.

Formation: Move the thumb side of the right "c" hand, palm facing left, across the upturned left palm from its base to the fingertips.

See also DIVINE, HOLY, ORTHODOX, PURE, RIGHTEOUS (A), SAINT, and SANCTIFY for other initialized signs formed in a similar manner.

CONVERT, CONVERSION, CHANGE, REFORM, REFORMATION

The hands seem to turn into something else, similar to the change that occurs in a person upon adopting a religion.

Formation: With the knuckles of the right "a" hand on the knuckles of the left "a" hand, palms facing each other, twist the wrists in opposite directions ending with the hands in reverse positions.

See also INTERPRET, REDEEM, and TRANSLATE for initialized signs formed in a similar manner.

COUNSELOR

This sign is a combination of a gesture indicating sending out advice and guidance and the person marker.

Formation: Move the right flattened "o" hand forward across the back of the left downturned flat hand, fingers pointing right, spreading the fingers into a "5" hand, palm down, as the right hand moves forward. Add the person marker.

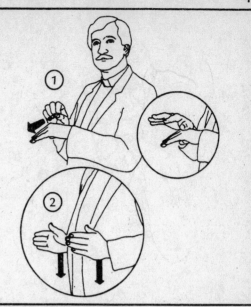

COVENANT (A)

The right hand takes an idea from the head and places it alongside another idea to indicate that they are the same.

Formation: Move the extended right index finger from pointing to the right side of the forehead, palm facing in, down and forward to beside the left extended index finger pointing forward in front of the chest, palm down.

Same sign for AGREE, AGREEMENT

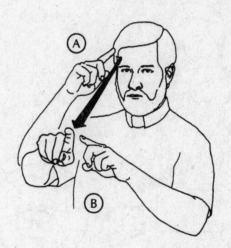

COVENANT (B)

This initialized sign indicates comparing one's ideas with another's and finding them to be in agreement.

Formation: Move the extended right index finger from pointing to the right temple, palm facing in, down and forward while changing into a downturned "c" hand, ending with it alongside the downturned left "c" hand in front of the chest.

48

COVET, JEALOUS, JEALOUSY, ENVY

This is a natural gesture of biting one's finger out of jealousy.

Formation: Put the tip of the bent extended index finger between the closed lips on the right side of the mouth, palm facing in.

See also DESIRE (A) (B) for an alternate sign and GREEDY for a sign with a related meaning.

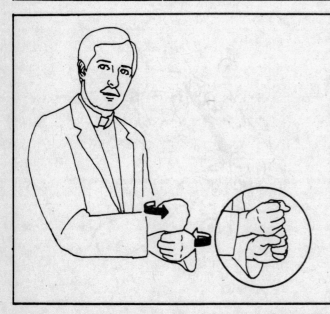

CREATE, MAKE, FORM

The hands seem to be molding a form, symbolizing God's causing the world and all things to exist.

Formation: With the right "s" hand on top of the left "s" hand, palms facing each other, twist the wrists in opposite directions several times, touching the hands together after each twist.

CREATION

This sign is a combination of GOD, CREATE, and WORLD.

Formation: Move the right "b" hand, palm left and fingertips pointing up and slightly forward, from above the head downward in an arc toward the face. Then with the right "s" hand on the top of the left "s" hand, palms facing each other, twist the wrists in opposite directions several times, touching the hands together with each twist. Bring the right "w" hand, palm left and fingers forward, in a circle over and around the left "w" hand, palm right and fingers forward.

Note: The first part of the sign may be formed with the open hand.

CREATOR, MAKER

This sign is a combination of GOD, CRE-ATE, and the person marker and refers to God's role in bringing the world and all things into existence.

Formation: Move the right "b" hand, palm left and fingertips pointing up and slightly forward, from above the head downward in an arc toward the face. Then with the right "s" hand on top of the left "s" hand, palms facing each other, twist the wrists in opposite directions several times, touching the hands together with each twist. Add the person marker.

Note: The first part of the sign may be formed with the open hand.

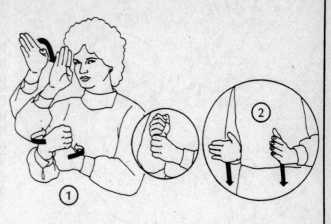

CROSS, CRUCIFIX

The hand outlines the shape of the traditional cross upon which Jesus Christ was crucified.

Formation: Move the right "c" hand, palm facing outward, first down from above the right side of the head to the right side of the body, then from left to right in front of the right shoulder.

See also EUCHARIST for an initialized sign formed in a similar manner.

CROWN, DIADEM

The fingers indicate the shape of a crown on the head.

Formation: Bring the curved thumb and middle fingers of both "5" hands down on top of both sides of the head, palms facing down.

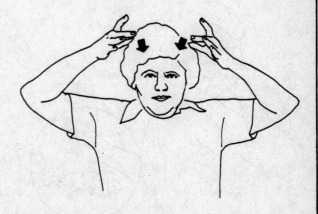

CRUCIFY, CRUCIFIXION

The hands mime the nailing of Christ's hands to the cross on Calvary followed by holding the hands out to display the nail-prints.

Formation: Strike the upturned left palm with the little finger side of the right "s" hand, palm left. Then strike the upturned right palm with the little finger side of the left "s" hand, palm right. Hold out the open hands, palms facing forward, up near each shoulder.

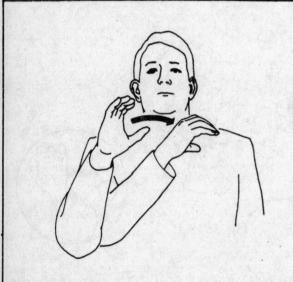

CULT (A)

This is an initialized sign formed with a movement similar to FALSE and refers to a religious body sharing an esoteric interest.

Formation: Move the right "c" hand, palm left, from the right side of the chin in an arc to the left, ending with the palm facing down.

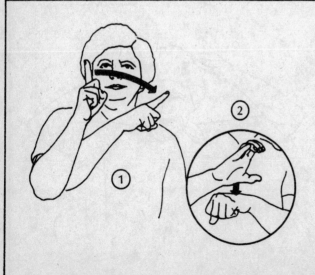

CULT (B)

This sign is a combination of FALSE and CHURCH and signifies a community of religious worship focusing upon a single ideal or principle.

Formation: Move the extended right index finger, palm left, from the right side of the nose outward to the left, striking the nose as it passes. Then tap the thumb side of the right "c" hand on the back of the left "s" hand, palm facing down.

CURSILLO

This initialized sign is formed similar to COURSE and signifies a short course reviewing doctrine or principles usually presented during a religious retreat.

Formation: Move the right "c" hand, palm facing out, from the fingertips to the base of the upturned left palm.

CUSTOM (A)

The hands move downward, a movement in American Sign Language that signifies a continued pattern, such as the practices handed down in the Jewish religion.

Formation: With the heel of the downturned right "s" hand on the back of the downturned left "s" hand, move both hands downward a short distance slowly.

CUSTOM (B)

This is an initialized sign formed with a downward movement, which in American Sign Language signifies continued activity.

Formation: With the right "c" hand, palm facing forward, on the back of the downturned left "s" hand, move both hands downward a short distance slowly.

52

DAMN, DAMNATION, DAMNED

This initialized sign is directed downward to the traditional location of hell.

Formation: Thrust the right "d" hand from the left chest, palm left and index finger pointing at an angle upward, downward and outward to the side of the waist, index finger pointing downward.

See also HELL (B) for an initialized sign formed in a similar manner.

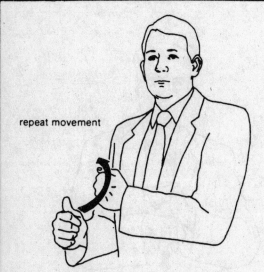

repeat movement

DANGER, DANGEROUS, PERIL

The right hand seems to threaten with hidden peril.

Formation: Brush the back of the right "a" thumb, palm left, upward several times on the back of the left "a" hand, palm toward the lower chest.

repeat movement

DAVEN, DAVENING

This sign mimes the movements of a person davening, that is, reciting the prescribed prayers in the daily and festival Jewish liturgies.

Formation: With the little-finger side of both cupped open hands close to the front of the chest, move the hands up and down slightly in rhythm with the head and shoulders bowing with them.

DAVID, KING DAVID

This initialized sign is formed like KING and indicates David's status as the second king of Judah and Israel from 1013 to 973 B.C.

Formation: Move the right "d" hand, palm facing left, from near the left shoulder down to the right hip.

Note: This sign is identical to the one used for DEACON; the meaning that is intended should be determined from the context.

See also CHRIST, KING, LORD (A), and MESSIAH for other initialized signs with similar meanings formed in a similar manner.

DEACON (A)

This initialized sign is formed like KING and refers to lay-assistants in the church.

Formation: Move the right "d" hand, palm facing left, from near the left shoulder down to the right hip.

Note: Since this sign is identical to one sign used for DAVID; the meaning that is intended should be determined from the context.

See also CHRIST, KING, LORD (A), and MESSIAH for other initialized signs formed in a similar manner.

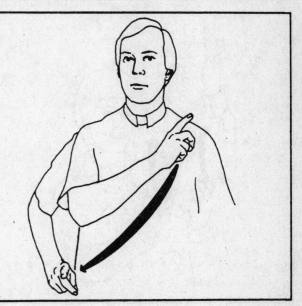

DEACON (B)

This initialized sign is formed like MEMBER. The sign refers to those people in the Roman Catholic Church who are clergy just below the rank of priest as well as those laypeople in other denominations who assist the pastor.

Formation: Touch the fingertips of the right "d" hand, palm toward chest, first near the left shoulder and then the right shoulder.

See also BOARD, BOARD OF DEACONS, and MEMBER for other initialized signs with related meanings formed in a similar manner.

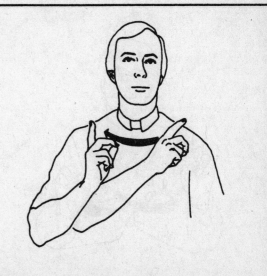

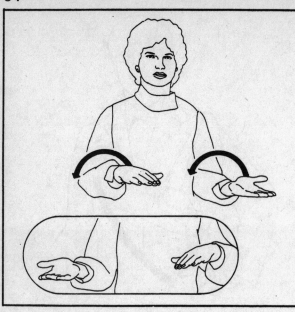

DEATH, DIE, DEAD, PERISH

The movement of the hands shows a body turning over and dying.

Formation: With the upturned right hand beside the downturned left hand, fingers pointing forward, side by side, flip the hands to the left so that the right palm faces down and the left palm faces up.

DEDICATE, DEDICATION

This initialized sign is made like OFFER and is used to refer to something set apart for religious use.

Formation: Beginning with both "d" hands, palms up, held in front of the chest, raise them to above the head while opening them into "5" hands.

See also OFFER and SACRIFICE for signs formed in a similar manner.

DELIVER, DELIVERANCE

This initialized sign is formed like SAVE and is used to designate man's release from the bondage of sin.

Formation: Bring both "d" hands, wrists crossed in front of the chest and palms facing in opposite directions, outward by twisting the wrists away from each other, ending with the palms facing forward in front of each shoulder.

See also REDEEM, REFORM, and SALVATION for initialized signs with related meanings formed in a similar manner.

DENY, DENIAL (A)

This is the sign NOT repeated several times for emphasis and signifies that one believes something not to be true.

Formation: Bring the thumbs of first the right hand and then the left hand from under the chin forward with a deliberate, repeated alternating movement.

Note: Both "a" hands may move forward simultaneously from under the chin in a strong single movement.

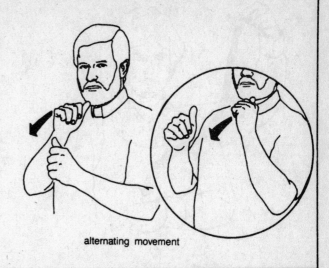

alternating movement

DENY, SELF-DENIAL (B)

The hands seem to be pushing down on inner desires.

Formation: Move both "a" hands, thumbs pointing down and palms facing out, down from in front of the chest a short distance.

Note: This sign may be formed with the right hand alone.

DENY, SELF-DENIAL (C)

The hand in this sign seems to squelch a built-up desire.

Formation: Bring the right "c" hand from under the chin, palm up, downward in front of the chest while changing into an "s" hand.

DESCEND (A)

The hand mimes a descending action.

Formation: Bring the right extended index finger from pointing down above the right shoulder in a wavy movement down to about waist level.

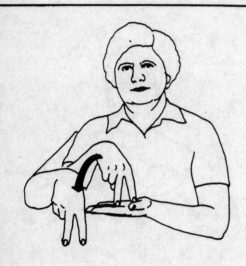

DESCEND (B)

The fingers represent a person standing on the ground and then descending, as in the descension of Christ into hell after his death.

Formation: Beginning with the fingertips of the inverted "v" right hand in the upturned flat left palm, move the fingers off the palm downward a short distance.

DESERVE, EARNED, WORTHY, MERIT

The hand seems to be gathering earned money together and refers to the rewards one gets because of one's own efforts.

Formation: Sweep the little-finger side of the right cupped "5" hand from the fingers to the heel across the upturned left hand, ending with an "s" right hand, palm toward the body.

Same sign for SALARY, INCOME

DESIRE, LONGING, WANT, (GOD'S) WILL, COVET (A)

The hands seem to bring something to yourself that you want.

Formation: Draw both upturned "claw" hands toward the body at waist level while constricting the fingers toward the palms.

See also COVET and WILL for alternate signs.

DESIRE, LONGING, WISH (B)

This sign is an exaggerated form of HUNGER and indicates an intense desire for something.

Formation: Move the fingertips of the right "c" hand, palm facing in, down on the chest from the throat downward.

See also COVET for a sign with a related meaning.

DESPISE, HATE, DISLIKE, DETEST

The fingers flick away something from the body that is distasteful. This is a directional sign that is formed toward the disliked person or object.

Formation: Flick the middle finger of both open hands, palms facing each other, off the thumbs outward from the body with a deliberate motion.

Note: This sign is usually accompanied by a distasteful look.

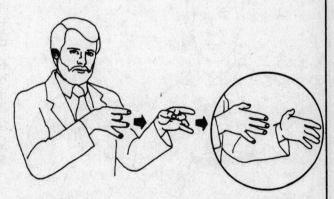

DEVIL, SATAN, DEMON

repeat movement

The fingers show the traditional conception of the horned devil, the major spirit of evil, ruler of Hell, and foe of God.

Formation: With the thumbs of both "3" hands touching the temples, palms facing forward, crook the extended index and middle fingers twice.

Note: This sign may be formed with one hand.

Same sign for MISCHIEF, MISCHIEVOUS

See also WICKED for a sign with a related meaning formed in a similar manner.

DEVOTED, DEVOTION

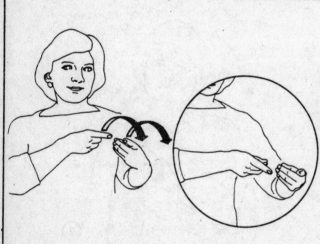

This initialized sign is formed like GIFT and symbolizes the giving of oneself to a religious cause or use.

Formation: Move both "d" hands, palms facing each other, from in front of the body forward in an arc.

See also GENUFLECT for an alternate sign and GIFT for a sign formed in a similar manner.

DIOCESE, DEPARTMENT

This initialized sign seems to encompass a defined area.

Formation: With the fingertips of both "d" hands touching each other, palms facing, move the hands around in a small circle, until the little fingers touch and the palms face the body.

See also CONGREGATION, ERUV, and SOCIETY for other initialized signs with related meanings formed in a similar manner.

DISCIPLE (A)

This is an initialized sign formed like FOLLOW and indicates one of the twelve companions of Christ who followed his teachings.

Formation: With the left "d" hand in front of the right "d" hand, palms facing forward, move both hands forward simultaneously in front of the body in double arcs.

DISCIPLE, APOSTLE, FOLLOWER (B)

This sign is a combination of FOLLOW and the person marker and signifies either the followers of Christ, the missionaries of the early Christian Church, or the members of the Mormon administrative council.

Formation: With the right "a" hand following the left "a" hand, palms facing toward each other, move both hands forward simultaneously in front of the body. Add the person marker.

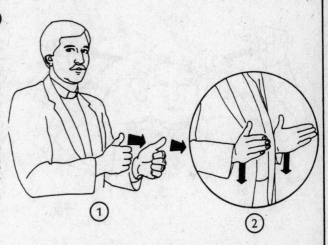

DISCIPLINE, PRACTICE, TRAINING

The motion of the hand demonstrates the repetitive nature of training that provides moral or mental improvement.

Formation: Rub the knuckles of the down-turned right "a" hand on the extended index finger of the left hand, palm facing in, with a repeated movement.

See also PUNISH for the verb form of DISCIPLINE.

repeat movement

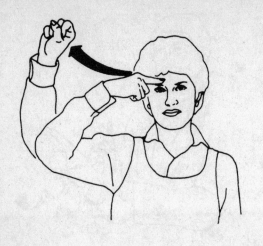

DISOBEY, DISOBEDIENCE, REBEL, REBELLIOUS (A)

This is a combination of THINK and a natural gesture for rebellion and signifies a disregard for God's commands.

Formation: Touch the extended right index finger to the forehead, palm toward the face. Then deliberately twist the wrist outward changing into an "s" hand as it moves upward and outward in an arc.

DISOBEY, DISOBEDIENCE (B)

The hands move with a rebellious gesture.

Formation: Beginning with the thumbs of both "a" hands on each side of the forehead, palms facing each other, move the hands deliberately upward and outward a short distance by twisting the wrists sharply.

DISTRICT (A)

This initialized sign inscribes an area signifying a designated region established for administrative purposes.

Formation: Bring the right "d" hand, palm facing down, from the back of the downturned left "s" hand, held in front of the chest, in a large counterclockwise circle, ending back where it began.

DISTRICT (B)

The hand encompasses a large area and signifies a jurisdiction designated for administrative purposes.

Formation: Beginning with the left downturned open hand held in front of the body, bring the right downturned open hand in a large arc from the right side of the body outward and back over the left hand.

See also DIOCESE for a sign with a related meaning.

DIVINE

This initialized sign is formed like CLEAN.

Formation: Drag the fingertips of the right "d" hand, palm down, across the upturned left palm from its base to off the fingertips.

See also CONSERVATIVE, HOLY, ORTHODOX, PURE, RIGHTEOUS (A) SAINT, and SANCTIFY for other initialized signs formed in a similar manner.

DIVINE PROVIDENCE

This sign is a combination of GOD and SUPERVISE and refers to divine direction or care provided by God.

Formation: Move the right open hand, palm facing left and fingertips pointing upward and slightly forward, in an arc toward the forehead and down in front of the face. Then with the little-finger side of the right "k" hand on the index-finger side of the left "k" hand, move them together in a circle in front of the body.

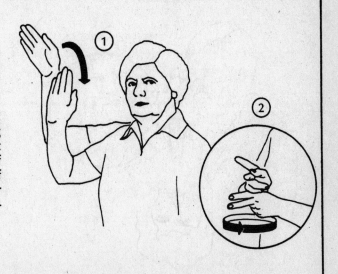

DIVORCE

This is an initialized sign showing an abrupt parting such as on the occasion of the dissolution of a marriage.

Formation: Begin with the fingertips of both "d" hands touching, palms facing each other. Then twist the wrists outward, jerking the hands apart, ending with the palms facing forward in front of each side of the body.

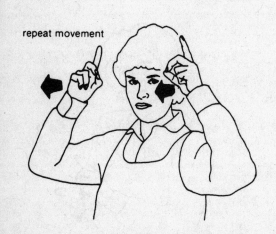

repeat movement

DOCTRINE, DOGMA

This is an initialized sign formed like TEACH and signifies religious principles that are taught.

Formation: Move both "d" hands, palms facing each other, from each side of the head forward with a short deliberate double motion.

See TEACH for a sign formed in a similar manner.

repeat movement

DOUBT, DISBELIEF, ATHEIST, (A)

This sign begins similar to BLIND and signifies being blind to an idea.

Formation: Bring the "v" fingers forward from pointing at each eye, palm toward face, crooking both extended fingers as the hand moves out.

Same sign for SKEPTICAL, CYNICAL

DOUBT (B)

This alternating movement in American Sign Language is used for concepts that seem to weigh the possibility of a fact being true.

Formation: Move both "a" hands, palms down, up and down in alternating movements in front of the body.

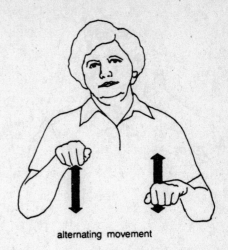

alternating movement

EARTH, EARTHLY, TERRESTRIAL

The movement of the hands represents the earth rotating on its axis.

Formation: While holding the back of the downturned left "s" hand with the thumb and middle finger of the downturned right hand, rock the right hand from side to side repeatedly.

See also UNIVERSE and WORLD for signs with related meanings.

repeat movement

EASTER, PASCHAL

This is an initialized sign formed like CELEBRATE and refers to the Christian festival commemorating Christ's resurrection.

Formation: Beginning with the palms of both "e" hands facing each other in front of each shoulder, twist the wrists to face the palms outward with a double motion.

Note: This sign may be done with one hand.

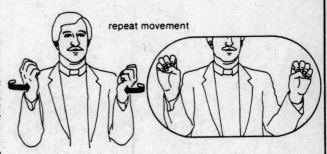

repeat movement

EGYPT

The finger demonstrates the serpent on the front of the headdress of Egyptian pharaohs.

Formation: Bring the knuckle side of the right ''x'' index finger against the center of the forehead.

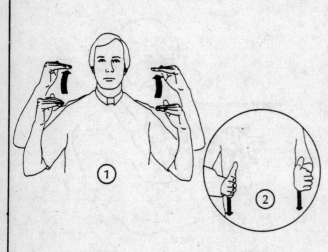

ELDER

This sign is a combination of HIGH and the person marker and refers to one of the governing officers of a church often having pastoral or teaching functions.

Formation: With both hands bent at right angles, palms facing each other and held near each shoulder, move them upward simultaneously, stopping abruptly at about eye level. Add the person marker.

EMMANUEL, IMMANUEL

This sign is a combination of GOD, WITH, and US, which is the translated meaning from the Hebrew. This is the name that the prophet Isaiah gave for the Messiah that was to come.

Formation: Move the right ''b'' hand, palm left and fingertips pointing up and slightly forward, from above the head downward in an arc toward the face. Then place both ''a'' hands together, palms facing each other. Next bring the fingertips of the right ''u'' hand from touching near the left shoulder, palm in, in an arc to in front of the right shoulder by twisting the wrist outward, ending with the palm facing forward.

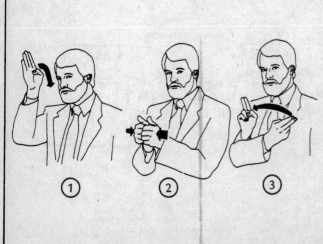

ENDURE, ENDURANCE, PATIENCE, PATIENT (A)

The thumb seems to silence a person to endure a burden.

Formation: Bring the thumbnail of the "a" hand, palm left, down from the lips to the chin very slowly.

Same sign for BEAR, TOLERATE

ENDURE, ENDURANCE, PRESERVE, LASTING, PERPETUAL (B)

The hands show moving something into the future with a continuing action.

Formation: With the right thumbtip on the left thumbnail, both palms facing down, move the hands forward in two small arcs.

Same sign for CONTINUE, KEEP ON, PERMANENT

See also PRESERVE for an alternate sign.

ENEMY, FOE

This sign is a combination of OPPOSITE and the person marker and indicates a person with opposing opinions.

Formation: Beginning with the tips of the horizontal index fingers pointing toward each other and touching in front of the body, palms facing in, pull them apart sharply. Add the person marker.

Note: This is a directional sign; change the orientation if you are the point of reference.

Same sign for OPPONENT, RIVAL

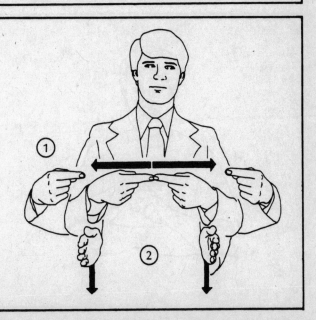

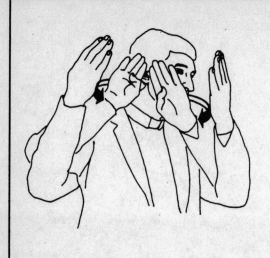

EPHPHATHA

The hands seem to remove a blockage from in front of the ears so one who is deaf may hear. Ephphatha is what Christ said as he caused a man who had been deaf from birth to hear again, and is translated as "Be opened."

Formation: Beginning with the back of both "b" hands held side by side against the right ear, fingertips pointing up, swing the hands outward and apart in arcs, stopping with the palms facing each other about a foot apart.

EPIPHANY, LIGHT

The hand represents a light going on and its rays spreading out. The sign is used to refer to the Christian festival held on January 6 to celebrate the manifestation of the divine nature of Christ to the Magi.

Formation: Beginning with the right thumb and fingertips touching near the right side of the head, palm facing in, twist the wrist outward while flicking the fingers open into a "5" hand, palm facing forward.

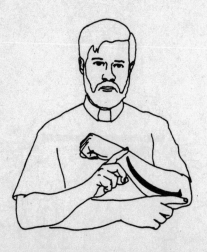

EPISCOPAL, EPISCOPALIAN, PROTESTANT EPISCOPAL

The finger follows the outline of the sleeve of a priest's surplice, worn by the clergy of the Episcopal Church, which separated from the Church of England in 1789.

Formation: With the extended right index finger, palm facing down, touch the wrist and then the elbow of the bottom of the left arm extended across the chest.

EPISTLE (A)

This is an initialized sign formed like LETTER and refers to the letters written by the Apostles and included in the New Testament.

Formation: Move the right "e" hand, palm toward the face, from the lips downward, landing in the upturned left palm.

EPISTLE (B)

This is a sign for LETTER and refers to the letters written by the Apostles to ancient churches.

Formation: Bring the thumb of the right "a" hand, palm facing left, from the lips downward to touching the thumbtip of the left "a" hand, palm facing the chest.

Same sign for LETTER, MAIL

ERUV

This initialized sign is formed like AREA and symbolizes the boundary line that establishes community limits for activities on the Sabbath.

Formation: Move both "e" hands, palms facing forward from together in front of the chest, apart and around in a small circle, coming together with the little fingers touching and the palms toward the body.

See also CONGREGATION, DIOCESE, and SOCIETY for other initialized signs with related meanings formed in a similar manner.

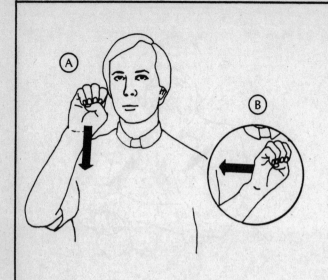

EUCHARIST

This initialized sign is formed like CROSS and refers to the Christian sacrament commemorating the Last Supper.

Formation: Move the right "e" hand, palm facing outward, first down from near the right side of the head to the right side of the body, then from left to right in front of the right shoulder.

See also COMMUNION (A)(B) for alternate signs.

See also CROSS for another initialized sign formed in a similar manner.

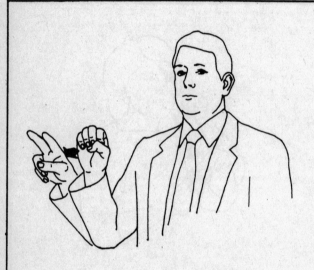

EVANGELISM, EVANGELICAL (A)

This initialized sign is an abbrevation formed like PREACH and signifies the spreading of God's word through missionary efforts.

Formation: Form an "e" with the right hand, palm forward, in front of the right shoulder. Then flick the index and middle fingers forward into a "v" hand.

See also PREACH for another sign formed in a similar manner.

repeat movement

EVANGELISM, EVANGELICAL (B)

This initialized sign is formed like PREACH and indicates zealous preaching of the gospel.

Formation: Move the right "e" hand, palm forward, above the right shoulder forward with several small jerky motions.

See also PREACH for a sign formed in a similar manner.

EVE

This initialized sign is formed at the lower part of the face, the location of female-designated signs. This is the name sign for Eve, the first woman and the wife of Adam.

Formation: Move the right "e" hand, palm facing forward, against the right side of the chin.

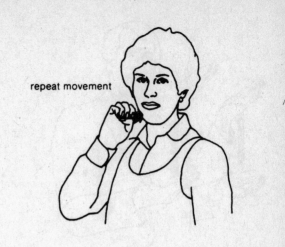

repeat movement

EVERLASTING, ETERNAL, ETERNITY, EVER, FOREVER, PERPETUAL, INFINITE, IMMORTAL

The sign is a combination of ALWAYS and STILL and indicates something of eternal duration, such as the infinite attributes of God.

Formation: Move the extended right index finger, pointing forward and palm up in a small circle clockwise in front of the right shoulder. Then move the right "y" hand, palm down, forward and upward in an arc, ending with the palm facing forward.

See also ALWAYS and INFINITE for alternate signs.

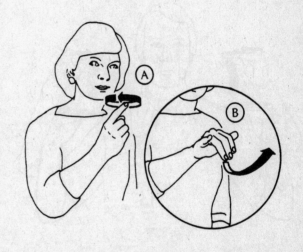

EVIL

This initialized sign is formed like BAD and seems to take something distasteful from the mouth and throw it outward such as something that is morally bad or wrong.

Formation: Beginning with the right "e" hand held near the mouth, palm left, turn the wrist and move the hand out and downward from the mouth with some force, ending with the palm facing down in front of the body.

See also BAD and WICKED for alternate signs with a similar meaning.

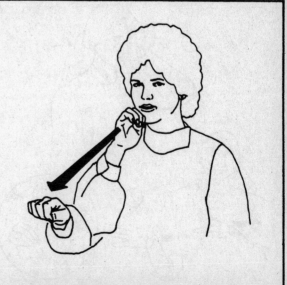

EXALT, EXALTATION, RAISE (A)

This sign is a natural gesture that signifies elevating God to a level of highest honor.

Formation: Move both upturned open hands from in front of the body straight upward in front of the face.

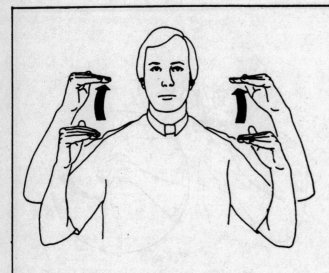

EXALT, EXALTATION, RAISE, SUPREME, SUPERIOR, HIGH (B)

The hands indicate a position at a higher level.

Formation: With both hands bent at right angles, palms facing each other and held near each shoulder, move them upward simultaneously, stopping abruptly at about eye level.

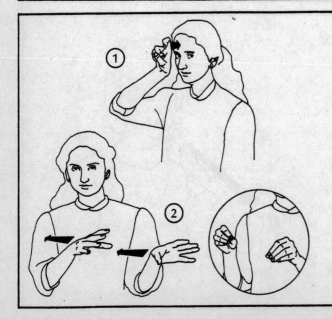

EXODUS

The sign is a combination of EGYPT and LEAVE and refers to the departure of the Israelites from Egypt after the captivity.

Formation: Bring the knuckle-side of the right "x" index finger against the center of the forehead. Then bring both downturned "5" hands from the left side of the body, the right hand nearer the body than the left hand, back toward the center of the body, drawing the fingers to the thumbs of each hand as they move.

FAITH, TRUST (A)

The sign is a combination of THINK and TRUST and indicates a conviction regarding religious doctrines without logical proof or material evidence.

Formation: Move the extended right index finger from the right side of the forehead down smoothly, changing into an "s" hand and landing on the left "s" hand in front of the chest, palms facing each other. See also TRUST for an alternate sign.

FAITH (B)

This sign is a combination of THINK and an initialized sign formed like TRUST.

Formation: Move the extended right index finger from the right side of the forehead down smoothly, changing into an "f" hand, and landing on the left "f" hand in front of the chest, palms facing each other.

FAITHFUL, LOYAL, LOYALTY

This is an initialized sign formed like REGULARLY and indicates the practicing members of a religious faith.

Formation: Tap the little-finger side of the right "f" hand on the thumb side of the left "f" hand, palms facing each other in a repeated motion while the hands move forward.

repeat movement

FALSE

The finger seems to push the truth aside.

Formation: Move the extended right index finger, palm left, from the right side of the nose outward to the left, striking the nose as it passes.

Same sign for ARTIFICIAL, COUNTERFEIT, FAKE

See also HYPOCRITE for a sign with a similar meaning.

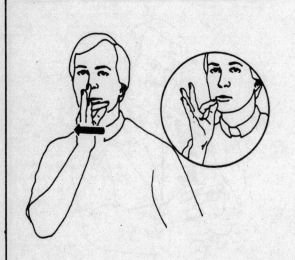

FAST, FASTING, ABSTAIN, ABSTINENCE (A)

This initialized sign seems to seal the lips to prevent eating, such as when abstaining from certain foods as a religious discipline.

Formation: Move the fingertips of the right "f" hand, palm left, from left to right across the lips.

See also YOM KIPPUR for an alternate sign.

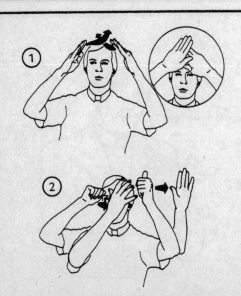

FATHER, HEAVENLY FATHER (A)

This sign is a combination of HEAVEN and FATHER and indicates the first person of the Trinity.

Formation: Starting with both open hands, palms facing each side of the head, move them toward each other crossing the right hand forward of the left in front of the forehead while turning the palms forward. Then with the right "a" hand at the forehead, palm left, and the left "a" hand somewhat forward, palm right, move both hands upward and outward toward the left while opening into "5" hands, palms facing out.

FATHER, HEAVENLY FATHER (B)

This is an exaggerated form of FATHER and refers to God the Father, the first member of the Trinity.

Formation: With the right "a" hand at the forehead, palm left, and the left "a" hand forward of the forehead, palm right, move both hands upward and outward toward the left while opening into "5" hands, palms facing out.

FEAR, AFRAID, FRIGHTENED (A)

This is a natural gesture protecting the body against something causing alarm or disquiet.

Formation: With the right "5" hand near the right shoulder and the left "5" hand on the lower left side of the chest, palms facing the chest and the fingers pointing toward each other, move both hands toward the center of the chest with a deliberate motion.

Same sign for SCARED, TERRIFIED, TERROR

FEAR, AFRAID, FRIGHTENED (B)

The hands quiver in alarm from something frightening.

Formation: Wiggle the fingers of both "5" hands, palms facing the chest and fingers pointing toward each other, while moving the hands toward each other with a short double movement.

Same sign for SCARED, TERRIFIED, TERROR

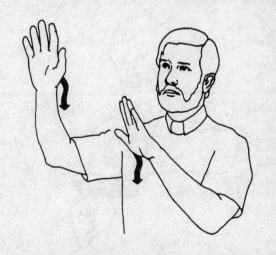

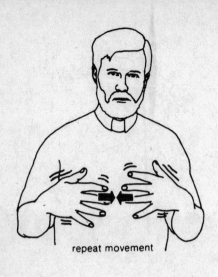

repeat movement

FEAR, DREAD, TERROR (C)

The hands are held up to protect the body against the unknown. This sign is used when referring to extreme reverence or awe of God.

Formation: Beginning with both raised "5" hands held on the right side of the body, right hand held higher than the left, palms facing outward, move both hands downward simultaneously with wavy movements.

Note: This is a directional sign toward the person or object to be feared.

alternating movement

FEAST

This is the repeated sign EAT and indicates the feasts held during religious festivals in honor of God.

Formation: With the thumb and fingertips of each hand together, palms facing in, bring the fingertips of each hand to the mouth repeatedly with alternating movements.

Same sign for BANQUET, MEAL, CONSUME

repeat movement

FELLOWSHIP

The hands show an interaction symbolizing the sharing of similar interests and beliefs among people of the same faith.

Formation: Circle the right "a" thumb, pointing downward, over the left "a" thumb, pointing upward.

Same sign for ASSOCIATE, EACH OTHER, MINGLE, ONE ANOTHER, SOCIALIZE

FLESH, MEAT (A)

The fingers grab a section of body tissue and symbolizes the meat of animals used in religious sacrifices.

Formation: Grasp the open left hand, palm facing the body, between the base of the thumb and the index finger with the thumb and index finger of the right hand, palm facing down.

See also MEAT AND DAIRY for a related sign.

repeat movement

FLESH, BODY (B)

The hands pat the body indicating the body, as distinguished from the mind or soul of man.

Formation: Touch the upper chest and then the lower chest with the palms of both open hands, fingers pointing toward each other.

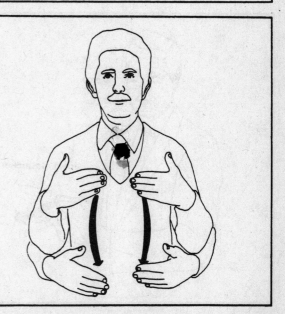

FLOOD

This sign is a combination of WATER and a gesture in which the hands mime the water's rising, as occurred during the universal deluge described in the Bible.

Formation: Touch the index finger of the right "w" hand, palm left, against the chin. Then raise both downturned "5" hands from in front of the body upward to chest level.

Note: The fingers may wiggle as the "5" hands are raised.

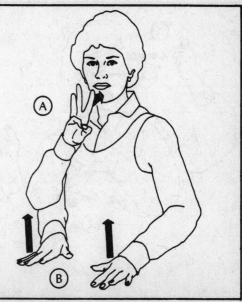

FORBID, FORBIDDEN

The finger strikes the other hand as a reprimand or warning to against an undesired action.

Formation: Strike the left open palm, facing right and fingers pointing forward, with the side of the extended right index finger, palm facing down.

Same sign for BAN, PROHIBIT

See also LAW (A) for a related sign formed in a similar manner.

repeat movement

FORGIVE, FORGIVENESS, PARDON, ABSOLUTION, DISPENSATION

The hand seems to brush away a fault or offense to free the offender from the consequences of it.

Formation: Brush the fingertips of the right downturned open hand across the fingertips of the left upturned open hand with a repeated movement.

Same sign for EXCUSE, PAROLE

See also ABSOLUTION for an alternate sign.

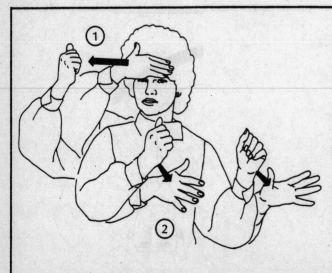

FORSAKE

This sign is a combination of FORGET and LEAVE and signifies abandoning and renouncing previous habits.

Formation: Bring the open hand, palm on forehead and fingers pointing left, across the forehead while closing into an "a" handshape near the right side of the head. Then with both "a" hands in front of the chest, thrust them forward while opening into "5" hands, palms down.

FOUNDED, INSTITUTED, ESTABLISH

The hand seems to take something and set it firmly in place such as establishing or setting up a practice.

Formation: Starting with the right "a" hand, palm facing out, above the left downturned hand, twist the right wrist forward, landing the little-finger side of the right "a" hand on the back of the left hand.

Same sign for APPOINT, APPOINTMENT

See also BEGINNING for a sign with a related meaning.

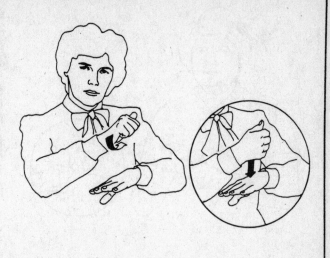

FREE WILL (A)

This sign is a combination of FREE and WILL and signifies the idea that man has the power to make choices, which are not predetermined by God.

Formation: Bring both "f" hands, wrists crossed in front of body and palms facing in, outward by twisting the wrists away from each other ending with the palms forward near the sides of the body. Then strike the index-finger side of the right "w" hand, palm facing forward, against the left palm, facing right with the fingers pointing up.

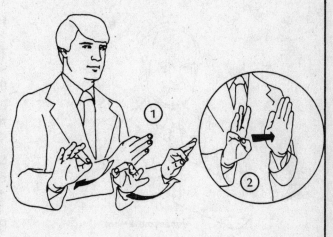

FREE WILL (B)

This sign is a combination of FREE and WANT and refers to the belief that man's choices in life are ultimately voluntary and not predetermined by God.

Formation: Bring both "f" hands, wrists crossed in front of the body and palms facing in, outward by twisting the wrists away from each other, ending with the palms forward near the sides of the body. Then draw both upturned "claw" hands toward the body at waist level while constricting the fingers toward the palm.

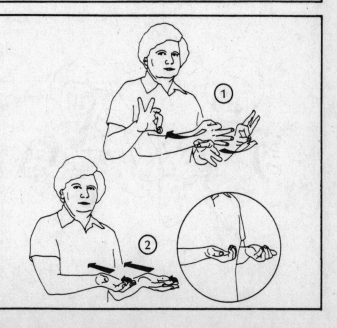

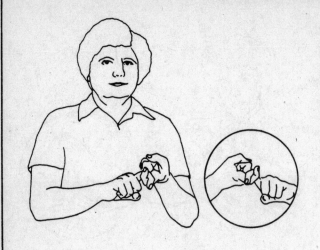

FRIEND, QUAKER, DISCIPLE

The fingers intertwine symbolizing the close relationship between companions.

Formation: Hook the right bent index finger down over the upturned left bent index finger. Repeat the action in reverse.

See also QUAKER and DISCIPLE for alternate signs.

repeat movement

FRUM, RELIGIOUS, OBSERVANT

The hand beats on the chest slowly as a sign of piety and refers to those Jews who observe the 613 commandments.

Formation: Knock the palm side of the right "a" hand against the left side of the chest with a small, slow movement.

See also YOM KIPPUR for a sign formed in a similar manner.

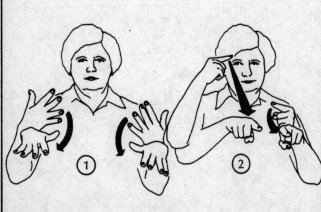

① ②

FULFILL, ACCOMPLISH, COMPLETE, FINISH

This sign is a combination of FINISH and AGREE and refers to the accomplishment of a prophecy as it was foretold.

Formation: Beginning with both "5" hands, palms facing the chest and fingers pointing up, twist the wrists sharply outward, ending with the palms facing down and the fingers pointing outward. Then move the extended right index finger from pointing to the right side of the forehead, palm facing in, down and forward to beside the left extended index finger pointing forward in front of the chest, palm down.

FUNDAMENTAL, FUNDAMENTALIST

This is an initialized sign formed like FOUNDATION and signifies the belief in the Bible as factual, historical record and incontrovertible prophecy.

Formation: Circle the right "f" hand, palm left and finger pointing forward, below the open left hand, palm down.

repeat movement

FUNERAL

The hands seem to portray a procession to the burial ceremony of the dead.

Formation: With the right "v" hand nearer to the body than the left "v" hand, palms facing forward and fingers pointing up, move both hands forward in short double arcs.

GENUFLECT, DEVOTED, DEVOTION

The fingers represent knees that are bending as in the custom, particularly in the Roman Catholic Church, of bending the knee in respect.

Formation: With the fingertips of the right "v" hand pointing down in the upturned left palm, bend the fingers downward at the knuckles.

See also DEVOTED for an alternate sign and KNEEL for a sign with a related meaning formed in a similar manner.

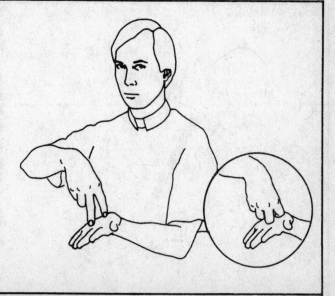

GIFT, CONTRIBUTION, PRESENT, AWARD, BESTOW

The hands seem to take something and present it to another person. This sign may refer to either a present or to a natural talent or aptitude. This sign is used as the noun form only.

Formation: Move both modified "a" hands, palms facing each other, from in front of the body, in a deliberate arc forward.

See also GIVE for the verb form of this sign and DEVOTE for an initialized sign formed in a similar manner.

GIVE, CONTRIBUTE, PRESENT, AWARD, BESTOW

The hands take something and present it to another.

Formation: Move both hands with the thumbs touching the fingertips and the palms facing up in front of the chest, upward and forward in an arc opening into upturned "5" hands.

Note: This is a directional sign toward whomever is the recipient of the gift. The beginning position may have the palms facing up or down. This sign may be done with the right hand only.

See also GIFT for the noun form of this sign.

GLORY, GLORIFY, GLORIOUS, MAJESTY

The hand mimes the rays that reflect from something of splendor. This sign refers to exalted honor as well as to the bliss of heaven.

Formation: Beginning with the right open palm across the upturned left open palm, bring the right hand upward toward the right shoulder, opening into a "5" hand and wiggling the fingers as the hand moves.

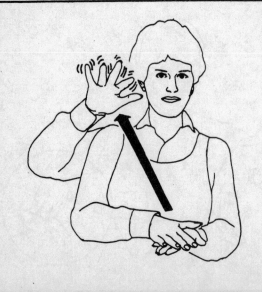

GOD, LORD, HASHAYM (A)

The sign is formed with a similar movement as HONOR and RESPECT, indicating God's position as the originator and ruler of the universe.

Formation: Move the right "b" hand, palm facing left and fingertips pointing up and slightly forward, in an arc toward the forehead and down in front of the face.

Note: This sign may be made with an open hand or a "g" hand instead of a "b" hand.

See also HONOR and RESPECT for initialized signs formed in a similar manner.

GOD, LORD, HASHAYM (B)

The finger points up to God and then moves down in a movement similar to RESPECT.

Formation: Beginning with the right extended index finger pointing up above the right side of the head, palm left, move the hand down in an arc toward the forehead and down in front of the face while changing a "b" hand, palm left and fingertips pointing up and slightly forward, and move it downward in an arc past the face.

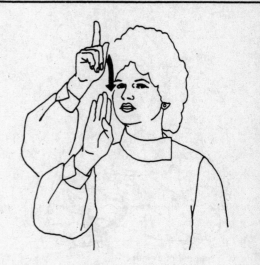

GOOD, WELL

The hand seems to take something desirable from the mouth and bring it forward.

Formation: Beginning with the fingertips of the right open hand on the lips, palm facing in, move the hand away and down from the mouth landing the back of the right hand in the upturned left open palm held in front of the body.

Note: The sign may stop after the right hand moves forward from the mouth.

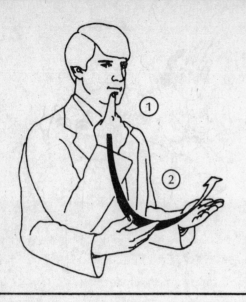

GOSPEL (A)

The sign is a combination of TELL and NEWS and refers to the first four books of the New Testament, describing the life, death, and resurrection of Jesus Christ.

Formation: Bring the right extended index finger from pointing at the lips, palm facing in, down in an arc while changing to a curved open hand, brushing the back of the right hand across the upturned left open palm.

repeat movement

GOSPEL (B)

This is an initialized sign formed like NEWS and refers to the narrative of Christ's life and teachings as presented in the first four books of the New Testament.

Formation: Bring the right "g" hand, palm left, across the upturned left palm from the fingers to the base with a repeated motion.

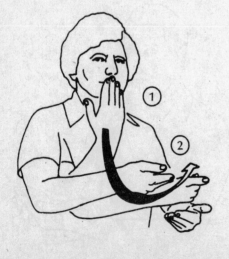

GOSPEL (C)

This sign is a combination of GOOD and NEWS and refers to the translation of *Gospel* from the Latin word meaning "good news."

Formation: Beginning with the fingertips of the right open hand on the lips, palm facing in, move the hand down in an arc while changing to a cupped open hand, brushing the back of the right hand across the upturned left cupped palm.

GRACE (A)

The hand seems to take something from God and shower it down, and signifies God's divine love being bestowed freely upon mankind.

Formation: Beginning with the right thumb touching the fingertips, palm facing forward above the right shoulder. Then twist the wrist inward, spreading the fingers while moving down to the right side of the head.

GRACE (B)

This is an initialized sign that indicates taking something from God and bringing it down to mankind.

Formation: Bring the right "g" hand from above the right shoulder, palm forward and fingers pointing up, downward in an arc, ending with the little-finger side against the left side of the chest.

GRACIOUS, BENEVOLENT, MERCY

This sign is a combination of GOOD and a modification of COMFORTABLE.

Formation: Move the right open hand from the lips, palm facing the body, down and forward over the left open hand, palm facing the chest and the fingers of both hands pointing toward each other in opposite directions. Then move the left hand up over the right hand exchanging places with it, keeping the hands close to the body.

Same sign for TENDER, GENTLE, KIND

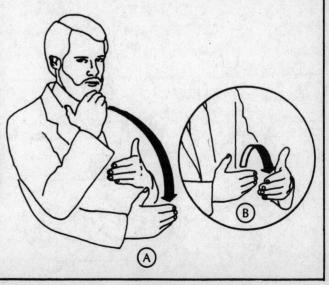

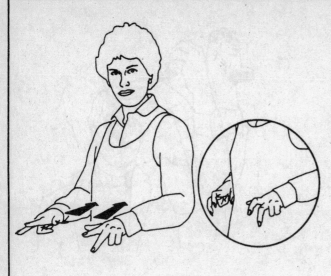

GREEDY, SELFISH

The hands seem to clutch at something, symbolizing an excessive desire to possess things.

Formation: With the "3" hands apart in front of the waist, palms down, draw the hands toward the body while crooking the fingers and thumbs.

See also See COVET for a sign with a related meaning.

GUIDE, LEAD

One hand pulls the other hand along, such as when a person shows another the way by leading, directing, or advising the course to be pursued.

Formation: Grab the fingertips of the left open hand, palm right, with the fingers of the right hand, palm toward the body. Let the right hand pull the left hand forward.

Note: This sign is sometimes formed by the right thumb and middle finger, grasping the left hand instead of the entire right hand.

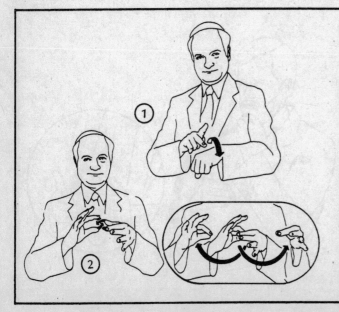

HAGGADAH

This sign is a combination of PASSOVER and STORY and refers to the book containing the story of the Exodus, read by Jewish people at their Passover seder.

Formation: Move the right "p" hand, palm down, from in front of the chest forward across the downturned left "s" hand. Link the thumbs and index fingers of both "f" hands and pull them apart with a repeated motion.

Note: The illustration shows PASSOVER (B) for the first part of the sign, however, PASSOVER (A) may be used, if preferred.

HALACHA (A)

This sign is a combination of JEW and LAW and refers to the legal elements of Talmudic literature that assist in interpreting the Scriptures.

Formation: With the open hand, palm toward the neck, draw the fingertips from the chin downward with a double motion, gathering the fingertips to the thumb as the hand moves. Then strike the right "I" hand on the left open palm, palms facing each other.

HALACHA (B)

This initialized sign is formed like LAW and refers to decrees, ordinances, and customs that comprise Jewish tradition.

Formation: Move the right "h" hand, palm down, across the left palm, facing right and fingers pointing up, touching first at the fingers and then the heel.

See also COMMANDMENTS, LAW, MOSES, and TESTAMENT for other initialized signs formed in a similar manner.

HASIDIM, CHASSIDIM

The fingers follow the shape of the long curls worn by certain observant Jewish sects.

Formation: Bring both extended index fingers from pointing up to each ear, palms facing back, downward, in a circling movement, ending near each side of the chest.

HEART (A)

The fingers outline the traditional shape of the heart near its physical location.

Formation: Use the extended index finger of both hands, palms toward body, to trace the outline of a heart on the left side of the chest.

HEART (B)

The middle fingers, considered the "feeling" fingers in American Sign Language, are used to form a heart shape. This sign is used for the emotional feelings of the heart, not for the physical organ.

Formation: Use the extended middle fingers of both hands, palms toward the body, to trace the outline of a heart on the left side of the chest.

HEAVEN, CELESTIAL, FIRMAMENT, PARADISE (A)

The hands indicate a global movement above the head signifying the firmament or traditional abode of God, the angels, and the souls of those already granted salvation.

Formation: Beginning with both open hands with the palms facing each side of the head, move them up toward each other over the head. As the hands meet at the top of the head, pass the right hand in front of the left while twisting both wrists outward, ending with both palms angled forward and upward, the right in front of the left, at angles.

Same sign for SKY, SPACE

HEAVEN, CELESTIAL, FIRMAMENT, PARADISE (B)

The hands seem to shield the body from the glory of God in heaven.

Formation: Starting with both open hands, palms facing each side of the head, move them toward each other crossing the right in front of the left in front of the forehead while turning the palms forward.

Same sign for SKY, SPACE

HEBREW

This sign is a combination of JEWISH and LANGUAGE and refers to the Semitic language of Israel.

Formation: With the right open hand, palm toward the neck, draw the fingertips from the chin downward with a double motion, gathering the fingertips to the thumb as the hand moves. Then beginning with the thumbs of both down-turned "I" hands touching in front of the waist, bring them apart in a double arc by twisting the wrists up and down.

repeat movement

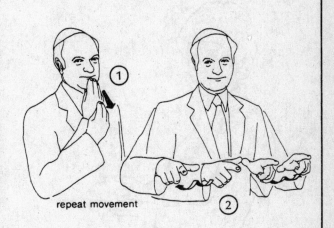

HELL, SHEOL, HADES (A)

This sign is the combination of a gesture pointing to the traditional location of hell and FIRE and signifies the place or state of torture and punishment for the wicked after death and is presided over by Satan.

Formation: Point the extended right index finger downward in front of the body. Then while wiggling the fingers of both "5" hands, move them in alternating circles upward, palms toward the chest.

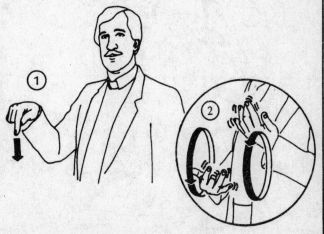

HELL (B)

This is an initialized sign directed toward the traditional location of hell and signifies the abode of condemned souls and devils.

Formation: Thrust the right "h" hand, palm facing left and fingers pointing forward, from the center of the chest downward and outward to the right side of the waist.

See also DAMN for an initialized sign formed in a similar manner.

HELP, ASSIST, AID

The right hand assists the left hand, symbolic of one who requires support during difficulty or distress.

Formation: Raise the left "a" hand, palm right, upward with the upturned right palm.

See also ADVOCATE for a sign formed in a similar manner.

HIGH HOLY DAYS

This sign is a combination of ADVANCED, HOLY, and DAY and refers to Rosh Hashanah and Yom Kippur, the days designated for religious observance for Jews.

Formation: Move both bent hands, palms facing each other, from in front of each shoulder, upward in a deliberate movement. Move the right "h" hand, palm facing the body, in a small circle in front of the chest and then across the upturned left palm from the base to off the fingertips. Place the elbow of the bent right arm, hand held straight up, palm left, on the downturned left hand. Move the extended right index finger downward toward the left elbow.

HOLY, HALLOWED, DIVINE, SACRED (A)

This is an initialized sign like CLEAN and designates anything worthy of worship or high esteem.

Formation: Form an "h" with the right hand near the base of the upturned left palm. Change to a flat right hand and wipe the palm of the right hand across the upturned left palm from its base to off the fingertips keeping the fingers perpendicular to each other.

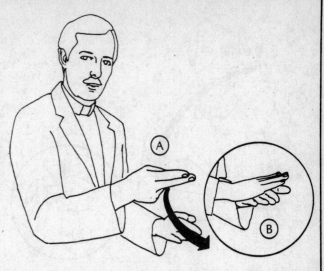

HOLY (B)

This is an initialized sign formed like CLEAN and refers to something set apart for a religious purpose.

Formation: Move the right "h" hand, palm facing the body, in a small circle in front of the chest and then across the upturned left palm from the base to off the fingertips.

See also CONSERVATIVE, DIVINE, ORTHODOX, PURE, RIGHTEOUS, SAINT, and SANCTIFY for other initialized signs formed in a similar manner.

HOLY (C)

This is an initialized sign formed like CLEAN and refers to something set apart as sacred.

Formation: Move the right "h" hand, palm facing the body, in a small circle in front of the chest. Change to a flat right hand and wipe the palm of the right hand across the upturned left palm from the base to off the fingertips keeping the fingers perpendicular to each other.

90

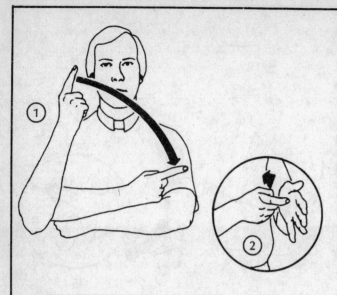

HOLY DAY OF OBLIGATION

The sign is a combination of DAY and RE-QUIRED and refers to those days that, according to the Roman Catholic Church should be observed by penitence and participation in a mass.

Formation: Place the elbow of the bent right arm, hand held straight up, palm left, on the downturned left hand. Move the extended right index finger downward toward the left elbow keeping the right elbow in place. Then with the fingertip of the right "x" index finger, palm left, against the open left palm, facing right, bring both hands toward the chest.

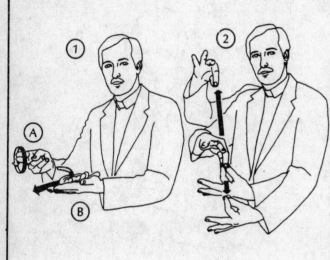

HOLY GHOST, HOLY SPIRIT

The sign is a combination of HOLY and SPIRIT and refers to the third person of the Trinity.

Formation: Move the right "h" hand, palm left, in a small circle in front of the chest. Change to a flat right hand and wipe the palm of the right hand across the left palm from its base to off the fingertips, keeping the fingers perpendicular to each other. Then touch the thumbs and index finger of both "f" hands to each other, right hand over left, palms facing. Draw the hands apart.

HONOR, HALLOWED, HAIL

This is an initialized sign formed like GOD and indicates the highest esteem, as for God.

Formation: Move both "h" hands, the right slightly higher than the left, palms facing each other and fingers pointing up, from above the head down in a slight arc toward the forehead and down to the chest.

Note: The head usually bows as the hands come down. This sign may be formed with only one hand.

See also GOD and RESPECT for signs with related meanings formed in a similar manner.

HOPE (A)

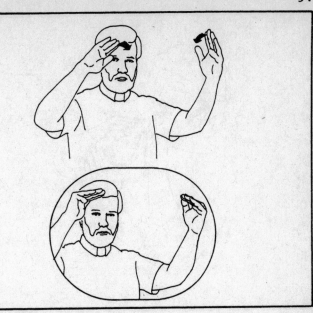

The hand seems to take a thought from the head and look to it in the future, as in anticipation of the Messiah's coming or for the Last Judgment.

Formation: With the right open hand near the right side of the forehead and the left open hand above the left shoulder, palms facing each other, bend the fingers down on both hands toward each other in a double motion.

See also EXPECT for a sign with a related meaning formed in a similar manner.

HOPE, EXPECT, EXPECTATION (B)

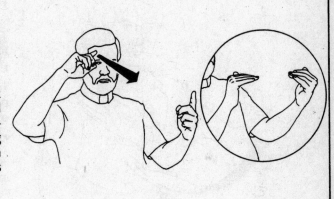

The hand seems to be looking in anticipation to something in the future, such as the coming of the Messiah or the Last Judgment.

Formation: With the right extended index finger near the right side of the forehead and the left extended index finger forward of the left shoulder, palms facing each other, bring the right finger down toward the left, changing into bent hands facing each other near the left shoulder.

Same sign for ANTICIPATE, ANTICIPATION

HOST

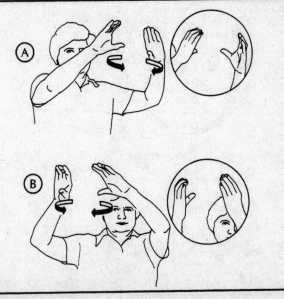

This is the sign GROUP formed in two locations above the head and refers to large groups of angels in heaven.

Formation: Move both "c" hands, palms facing each other, above the left side of the head, in a circular movement outward. Repeat the same movement above the right side of the head.

HUMBLE, HUMILITY, MEEK, LOWLY

One hand moves to a position beneath the other and indicates deferential respect and an awareness of one's shortcomings.

Formation: Bring the right "b" hand, palm left, from the chin in an arc forward and under the left downturned open hand held in front of the face.

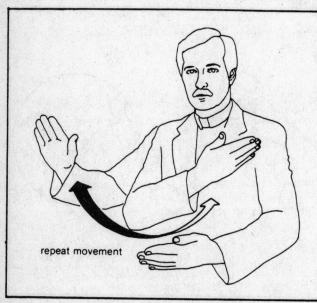

repeat movement

HYMN, SONG, ANTHEM

The hand follows a rhythmic movement indicating a song, as one intended for the praise and worship of God.

Formation: Swing the right open hand, palm left, back and forth in a large arc over the extended upturned left arm.

Same sign for MUSIC, MELODY

See also CANTOR, CHOIR, and PSALM for initialized signs formed in a similar manner.

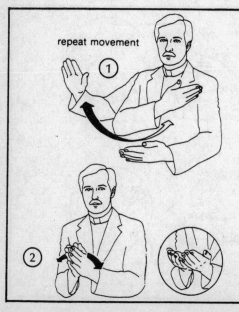

repeat movement

①

②

HYMNAL, HYMNBOOK

The sign is a combination of SONG and BOOK and refers to a collection of church hymns.

Formation: Swing the right open hand, palm left, back and forth in a large arc over the extended upturned left arm. Then starting with both palms together in front of the chest, fingers pointing forward, move the hands apart at the top, keeping the little fingers together.

HYPOCRITE, HYPOCRISY

The hands seem to cover up something not meant to be exposed and refers to a person who espouses beliefs that are not sincerely held.

Formation: With the right open on the back of the left open hand, both palms facing down in front of the body, the right fingers bend down pushing on the left fingers, bending them down.

Same sign for IMPOSTER, FAKE

See also FALSE for a sign with a similar meaning.

HYSSOP, ASPERGILLUM

The hands mime holding a aspergillum which is used for sprinkling in certain Hebraic and Catholic purification rites.

Formation: Move the right modified "a" hand, palm left, first from in front of the right shoulder downward and forward with a deliberate movement and then repeated from the left side of the chest.

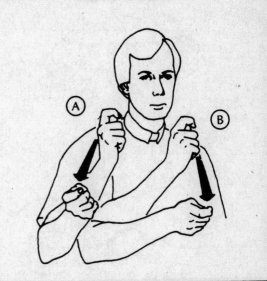

IDOL, GODS, IMAGE

This initialized sign follows the shape of a graven image used for worship.

Formation: With both "i" hands held on each side of the head, palms facing each other, bring them downward in a wavy movement to in front of the body.

See also STATUE for a sign with a related meaning formed in a similar manner.

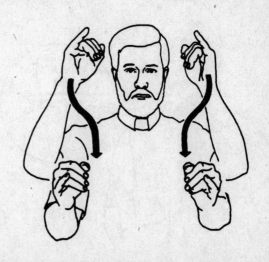

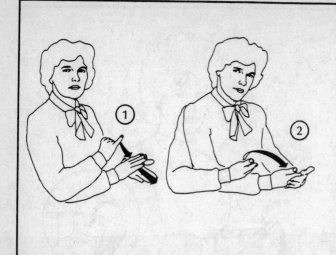

IMMACULATE CONCEPTION (A)

This is a combination of an initialized sign formed like CLEAN and BORN and signifies the Roman Catholic doctrine that the Virgin Mary was conceived in her mother's womb free from sin.

Formation: Form an "i" with the right hand near the base of the upturned left palm. Change to a flat right hand and wipe the palm of the right hand across the left palm from its base to off the fingertips, keeping the fingers perpendicular to each other. Then bring the right open hand, from the palm on the stomach, outward, landing palm up on the upturned left palm.

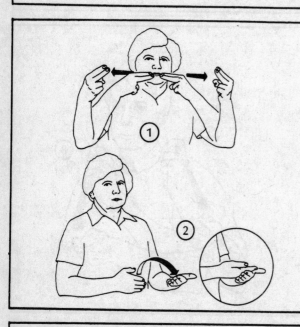

IMMACULATE CONCEPTION (B)

This sign is a combination of INNOCENT and BIRTH.

Formation: Move both "u" hands from touching the lips, palms toward the face, down and outward, ending with the hands in front of each shoulder, palms facing up and fingers pointing upward. Then bring the right open palm from the stomach outward, landing palm up on the upturned left palm.

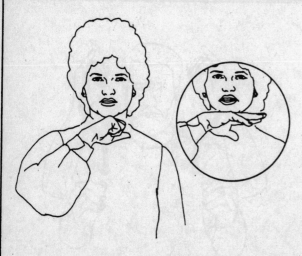

IMPURE, FILTHY, SOILED, STAINED, DIRTY, DEFILED

This sign is formed like PIG and is used to specify something that is in a state of immorality and sin.

Formation: With the back of the right "s" hand, palm down, under the chin, open the fingers deliberately into a "5" hand.

INCARNATE, INCARNATION (A)

This is an initialized sign formed like BORN and signifies the embodiment of God in the human form of Jesus.

Formation: With the back of the right "i" hand across the upturned left "i" hand, both palms facing up, move both hands forward a short distance.

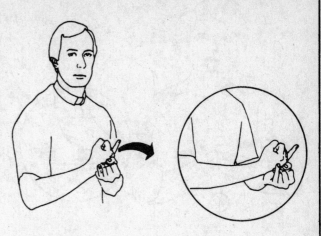

INCARNATE, INCARNATION (B)

This sign is a combination of BECOME and BODY and refers to Jesus Christ's assuming a human body.

Formation: With the right open palm against the left open palm, twist the wrists to put the hands in reverse positions. Then touch the upper chest and then the lower chest with the palms of both open hands.

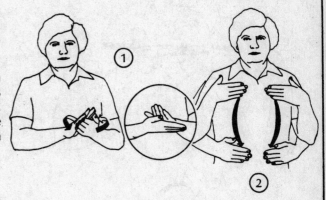

INCENSE, CENSER

The hands mime holder a CENSER, the vessel containing incense, a fragrant substance that is burnt in religious worship.

Formation: With the left "s" hand held with the palm facing toward the upper chest, swing the right "s" hand in and out under it, palm toward body and then down.

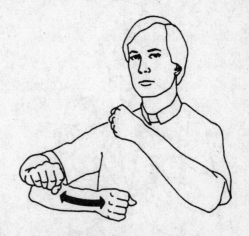

repeat movement

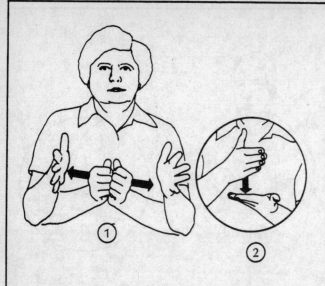

INFINITE

This sign is a combination of WITHOUT and STOP and refers to God's attribute of existing without beginning or end.

Formation: Beginning with the knuckle side of both ''a'' hands together, palms facing each other, pull the hands apart abruptly while opening into ''5'' hands, stopping in front of each side of the chest, palms facing each other and fingers pointing forward. Then bring the little-finger side of the right open hand, palm left, down sharply on the upturned left open palm.

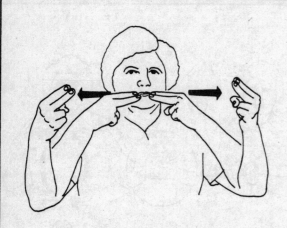

INNOCENT, BLAMELESS, SINLESS

The sign is used to refer to someone who is uncorrupted by wrongdoing.

Formation: Move both ''u'' hands from touching the lips, palms toward the face, downward and outward, ending with the hands in front of each shoulder, palms facing up and fingers pointing forward.

INSPIRE, INSPIRATION, FILLED WITH

Some internal force seems to rise in the body, as when a person becomes able to communicate because of divine influence.

Formation: Beginning with the thumbs touching the fingertips of each hand in front of the waist, palms facing in and fingers pointing up, bring the hands up in front of the chest, spreading the fingers into ''5'' hands as they move.

INSTALL, INSTALLATION, CONFIRMATION

The hands mime blessing the head of the person assuming a religious office.

Formation: Place the downturned palms on top of each side of the head, fingers pointing back.

See also CONFIRMATION (A) (B) and ORDAIN for signs with related meanings.

INTERPRET, INTERPRETATION (A)

The sign is formed like CHANGE and indicates the process of explaining or simplifying the Bible so it is understandable to the layperson.

Formation: Touch the thumbs and fingers of both "f" hands, palms facing each other. Twist the wrists in opposite directions with alternating movements toward and away from the body.

See also CONVERT, REPENT, and TRANSLATE for signs formed in a similar manner.

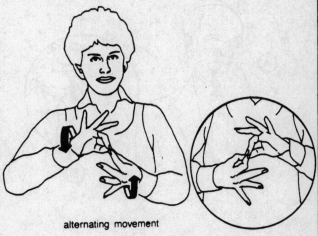

alternating movement

INTERPRET, INTERPRETATION, EXPLAIN, EXPLANATION (B)

This sign is used for explaining a Biblical reference for the purpose of clarifying it.

Formation: Move both "f" hands forward and back with an alternating movement, palms facing each other, in front of the body.

alternating movement

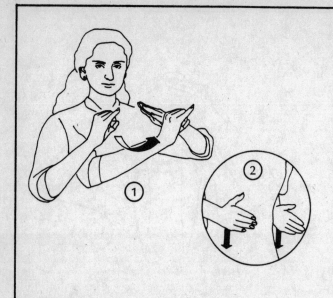

ISAIAH

This initialized sign is formed like PROPHET and identifies Isaiah, a Judaean prophet of the eighth century B.C. who foretold the Messiah's coming.

Formation: Move the right "i" hand, palm facing left, from in front of the chest forward in an arc under the downturned left open hand, held in front of the chest. Add the person marker.

See also PROPHET for a sign formed in a similar manner.

ISRAEL

This is an initialized sign that indicates a traditional Jewish beard and refers to the homeland of many Jewish people.

Formation: Bring the right extended little finger, palm toward face, down first on the left side of the chin and then on the right side of the chin.

ISRAELITES, HEBREWS

The sign is a combination of JEWISH and PEOPLE.

Formation: With the "5" hand, palm toward the neck, draw the fingertips from the chin downward with a double motion, gathering the fingertips to the thumb as the hand moves. Then using both "p" hands, circle outward with alternating movements, palms facing each other.

JEHOVAH'S WITNESSES

This is an initialized sign that refers to the religious sect formed in the late nineteenth century characterized by active evangelism and the belief in the imminent approach of the millenium.

Formation: Form a "j" with the right hand near the right shoulder. As the hand completes the "j" change to a "w" hand, palm facing back.

JERUSALEM (A)

This is a combination of an initialized sign and TOWN and is used to designate the town in ancient Israel whose temple was dedicated to the worship of God.

Formation: Form a "j" with the right hand near the right shoulder. Then with palms facing and hands held at a slight angle, tap the fingertips together first in front of the left side of the chest and then again in front of the right side of the chest.

See also BETHLEHEM and NAZARETH for initialized signs formed in a similar manner.

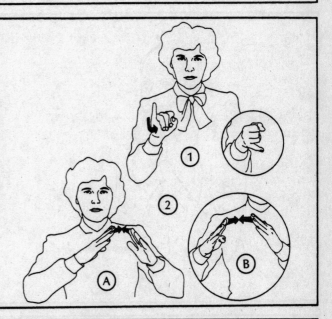

JERUSALEM (B)

The hand mimes kissing the mezuzah, located on the doorposts of many Jewish homes or other buildings in Israel.

Formation: Pat the fingertips of the right open hand first against the lips and then forward with the palm facing forward.

See also MEZUZAH for a sign with a related meaning formed in a similar manner.

JESUS

The fingers point out the nailprints in Jesus's hands. Jesus is regarded by Christians as the Messiah and the second member of the Trinity.

Formation: Touch the bent middle finger of the right "5" hand into the center of the left open palm, palms facing each other. Reverse the action by touching the bent middle finger of the left "5" hand into the right open palm.

repeat movement

JEWISH, JEW, HEBREW

The hand follows the shape of a traditional Jewish beard.

Formation: With the cupped right hand, palm toward the neck, draw the fingertips from the chin downward with a double motion, gathering the fingertips to the thumb as the hand moves.

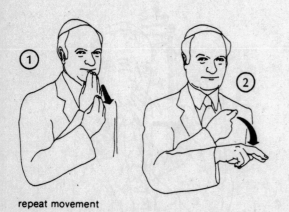

repeat movement

JUDAISM

This sign is a combination of JEW and RELIGION and designates the monotheistic religion of Jewish people, which traces its origins to Abraham.

Formation: With the right cupped hand, palm toward the neck, draw the fingertips from the chin downward with a double motion, gathering the fingertips to the thumb as the hand moves. Then touch the fingertips of the right "r" hand to the left chest, palm facing the body. Move the "r" smoothly down and outward, ending with the palm facing left and the finger pointing down.

JUDGMENT, JUDGE, CONDEMN, TRIBUNAL (A)

The hands seem to weigh a decision on the traditional balance of justice, as at God's final reckoning on Judgment Day.

Formation: With both "f" hands apart but facing each other, fingers pointing forward, move them with an alternating movement up and down in front of each side of the body.

See also CONDEMN for an alternate sign.

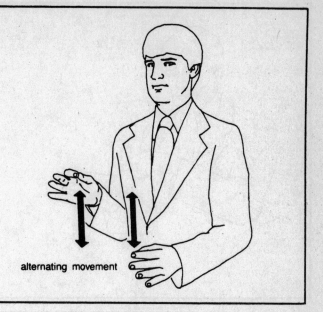

alternating movement

JUSTIFICATION

This sign is a combination of JUDGE and EQUAL and refers to the doctrine in which God judges believers as righteous despite sinful living.

Formation: With both "f" hands apart but facing each other, fingers pointing forward, move them with an alternating movement up and down in front of each side of the body. Then tap the fingertips of both bent hands together, palms facing each other, in front of the chest.

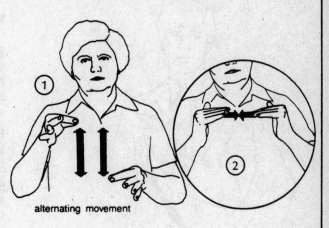

alternating movement

KIDDUSH

The hand seems to hold an overflowing cup of wine over which the kiddush blessing is made for the Sabbath and festivals.

Formation: Bring the upturned right cupped hand straight upward in front of the right side of the body.

KILL, SLAY, MURDER

The finger makes a jabbing motion as if stabbing someone.

Formation: Push the extended right index finger, palm down, forward and down under the left downturned open palm.

KING

This initialized sign follows the shape of the sash worn by royalty and is used to refer both to the Old Testament monarchs and to Christ's designation as King of the Jews.

Formation: Move the right "k" hand, palm left, from the left shoulder down to the right hip.

See also CHRIST, DAVID, LORD, and MESSIAH for other initialized signs formed in a similar manner.

KINGDOM

This initialized sign is a combination of KING and a gesture showing an area of land and designates the realm of God's eternal spiritual sovereignty.

Formation: Move the right "k" hand, palm left, from the left shoulder down to the right hip, where the hand changes to an open hand and moves upward in an arc to circle over the downturned left hand.

KNEEL

The fingers represent bended knees, a position of respect before God.

Formation: Place the knuckles of the bent right "v" fingers, palm facing the body, in the upturned left palm.

See also GENUFLECT and PROTESTANT for signs with related meanings formed in a similar manner.

KOSHER

This is an initialized sign and indicates that something conforms to the Jewish dietary laws and is properly prepared for eating.

Formation: Shake the right "k" hand, palm left, back and forth from the wrist in front of the chest.

Note: Usually the mouthed word *kosher* accompanies the sign.

repeat movement

LAW (A)

This initialized sign is formed like FORBID and signifies God's rules for mankind.

Formation: Strike the right "l" hand on the left open palm, palms facing each other.

See also FORBID for sign with a related meaning formed in a similar manner.

LAW (B)

This is an initialized sign and signifies the recording of laws on a tablet or book.

Formation: Move the right "l" hand across the left open palm, touching first at the fingers and then at the heel, palms facing each other.

See also COMMANDMENTS, HALACHA (A), MOSES, and TESTAMENT for other initialized signs formed in a similar manner.

alternating movement

LAYPERSON, LAITY, PARISHIONERS, MANKIND, PEOPLE, HUMANITY

This is the sign for PEOPLE and is used to refer to the members of a congregation as distinguished from the clergy.

Formation: Using both "p" hands, palms facing down, circle them outward with alternating movements.

Note: The hands may circle inward instead.

See also PERSONAL for the singular form of this sign.

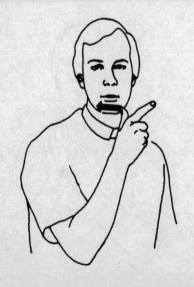

LENT

This is an initialized sign formed like FAST and indicates abstinence from a chosen substance during the Lenten season—the forty days before Easter—as a gesture of penitence.

Formation: Move the thumbtip of the right hand, palm left, across the chin from left to right.

See also FAST for another initialized sign formed in a similar manner.

LESSON

The left hand represents a page and the right hand designates a portion of it.

Formation: Touch the little-finger edge of the right cupped hand, palm toward body, first on the fingers and then on the heel of the upturned left hand, fingers pointing out.

LIE, FALSEHOOD, UNTRUTH (A)

The finger's movement shows talking out of the side of the mouth.

Formation: Push the right extended index finger, palm facing down, across the chin from right to left.

See also FALSE for a sign with a related meaning.

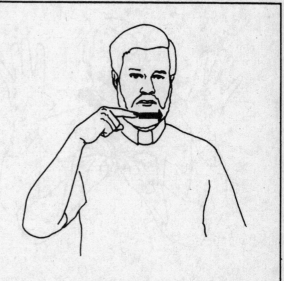

LIE, FALSEHOOD, UNTRUTH (B)

The hand shoves the truth to the side of the mouth and symbolizes any false information deliberately presented as being true.

Formation: Push the index-finger edge of the downturned right "b" hand across the chin from right to left with a deliberate movement.

See also FALSE for a sign with a related meaning.

LIFE, LIVING, MORTAL

The sign symbolizes vitality surging through the body.

Formation: Bring both "I" hands, palms toward the body and index fingers pointing toward each other, upward from the waist to the chest.

See also LIVE for the verb form of this sign.

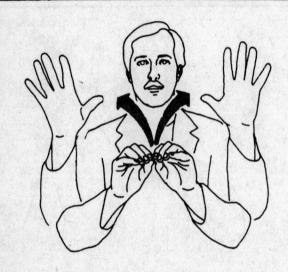

LIGHT, LUMINOUS, BRIGHT

The hands seem to clear away any haze in front of the eyes.

Formation: Starting with the fingertips touching the thumbs, palms facing forward and near each other, move the hands upward and apart, opening into "5" hands in front of each shoulder.

Same sign for CLEAR, OBVIOUS

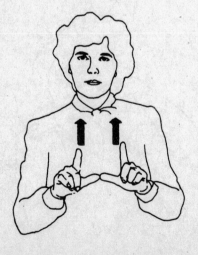

LITURGY

This is an initialized sign formed like MASS and refers to the rites of worship.

Formation: With the thumbtips of both hands touching in front of the chest, palms facing out, lift the hands upward in front of the face.

See also MASS for another sign formed in a similar manner.

LIVE, DWELL, EXIST

This sign symbolizes vitality surging through the body.

Formation: Bring both "a" hands with the thumbs extended upward, palms toward the body, upward from the waist to the chest.

Same sign for ALIVE, ADDRESS, SURVIVE, RESIDE

See also LIFE for the noun form of this sign.

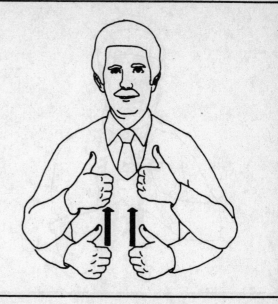

LORD (A)

This is an initialized sign that follows the shape of the sash worn by royalty and refers to Christ's designation as the King of the Jews.

Formation: Touch the thumb of the right "l" hand, palm left and index finger pointing outward at an angle, first to the left shoulder and then to the right hip.

See also CHRIST, DAVID, KING, and MESSIAH for other initialized signs formed in a similar manner.

LORD (B)

This is an initialized sign that gestures dramatically upward toward the traditional location of heaven. This sign is poetic and is often used in music.

Formation: Touch the thumb of the right "l" hand, palm facing left and index finger pointing outward at an angle, to the left shoulder. Swing the right hand outward and upward in a large arc, ending above the right side of the head with the palm facing out and the index finger pointing up.

LOVE, DEAR

This is a natural sign for holding someone or something very dear near the heart.

Formation: Cross the arms of both "a" hands at wrists, palms toward body, across the chest.

Same sign for HUG.

See also BELOVED for an alternate sign.

LULAV

The left hand seems to hold the *etrog* (lemon) and the right hand holds the *lulav* (palm), symbolic of the festival of Sukkoth, which commemorates the temporary shelter of the Jews in the wilderness.

Formation: With the right hand cupped tightly over the left "a" hand, palms facing each other, shake both hands first on the left side of the waist, then on the right side of the waist, and finally over the right shoulder.

LUTHER

This is an initialized sign used to designate Martin Luther, a sixteenth-century German monk known as the founder of Protestantism.

Formation: Tap the thumbtip of the right "l" hand in the center of the chest, palm left and index finger pointing outward at an angle.

See also LUTHERAN (A) for an alternate sign.

LUTHERAN, LUTHER (A)

This is an initialized sign and indicates Luther's nailing the Ninety-five Theses to the church door at Worms, Germany, an act that led to a separation from the Roman Catholic Church and the establishment of the Lutheran Church.

Formation: Tap the thumbtip of the right "l" hand, palm facing forward, against the palm of the open left hand, palm facing right.

LUTHERAN (B)

This is an initialized sign formed like CHURCH.

Formation: Tap the heel of the right "l" hand, palm facing forward, on the back of the downturned left "s" hand. Then tap the right "s" hand on the back of the downturned left "s" hand.

See also CATHEDRAL, CHURCH, PARISH, PETER, SYNAGOGUE, and TEMPLE for other initialized signs formed in a similar manner.

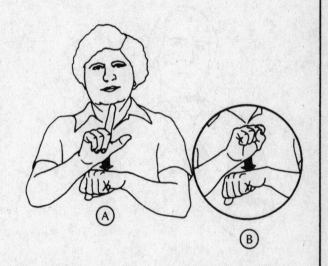

MANGER

The fingers form the shape of the traditional manger in which the baby Jesus was laid.

Formation: Thrust the middle finger of the right "v" hand between the index finger and middle finger of the left "v" hand, palms facing each other.

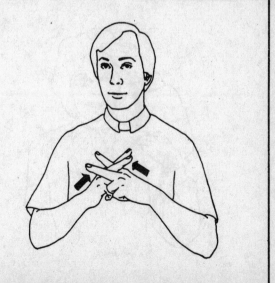

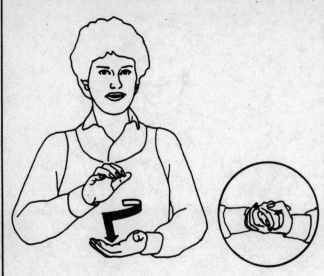

MARRIAGE, MARRY, HOLY MATRIMONY, NUPTIALS

This sign demonstrates the joining of hands that is symbolic of the union of marriage.

Formation: Begin with both cupped hands a few inches apart, palms facing and the right hand above the left. Bring the right hand down in a small circular motion until the hands clasp.

See also WEDDING for the sign referring to the marriage ceremony.

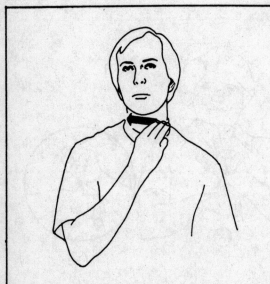

MARTYR

The fingers seem to behead a person in this initialized sign, which is used to refer to anyone who endures extreme suffering, even death, because of religious beliefs.

Formation: Move the fingertips of the right "m" hand, palm down, across the neck from left to right.

MARY, VIRGIN MARY (A)

This is an initialized sign that follows the shape of the veil covering the head of Mary, the mother of Jesus.

Formation: Bring the right "m" hand, palm toward the head, from the top of the right side of the head down to the right shoulder.

Note: This sign may be formed with both "m" hands on each side of the head.

MARY, VIRGIN MARY (B)

This is an initialized sign using the letters V and M and follows the shape of the veil covering the head of the Virgin Mary.

Formation: Bring the right "v" hand, palm right, from the left shoulder across the top of the head, changing into an "m" as it moves over the head, ending on the right shoulder, palm down.

MASS, HOST

The fingers indicate lifting the Host as the priest does during a Roman Catholic Mass.

Formation: With the thumb and index fingertips of both "f" hands touching in front of the chest, palms facing, lift the hands upward in front of the face.

See also LITURGY for an initialized sign formed in a similar manner.

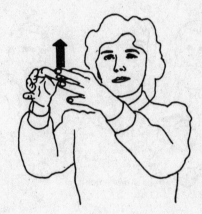

MASTER

This initialized sign is formed similar to OVER and indicates the Lord's authority over all things.

Formation: Move the right "m" hand, palm down, in a large circle over the downturned left open hand.

See also DISTRICT (A) (B) and KINGDOM for signs formed in a similar manner.

MATZOTH

This is the sign CRACKER and refers to the matzoth, the unleavened bread eaten by Jews during Passover.

Formation: Knock the palm side of the right "a" hand above the elbow of the bent left arm held across the chest.

Same sign for CRACKER

MEAT AND DAIRY, MILCHIG AND FLAYSHIG

repeat movement

This sign is a combination of MEAT and MILK and signifies those foods that are forbidden by Jewish dietary laws to be eaten together.

Formation: Grasp the left hand between the base of the thumb and the index finger with the thumb and index finger of the right hand and move both hands back and forth toward the chest with a repeated movement. Then with the "c" right hand near the right shoulder, palm left, close the hand into an "s" shape repeatedly.

MEDITATE, MEDITATION

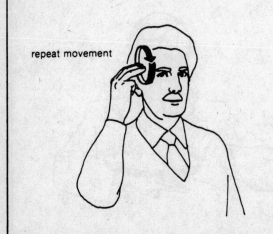

repeat movement

This initialized sign is formed like CONSIDER and represents the devotional exercise of contemplation.

Formation: Move the right "m" hand, palm toward the face, in a small circle near the right side of the forehead.

See also PONDER for a sign with a similar meaning formed in a similar manner.

MEETING, CONVENTION, CONFERENCE, CONVOCATION, ASSEMBLY, GATHERING

The fingers represent people coming together.

Formation: With the thumbs of both "5" hands touching, palms facing each other, tap the other fingertips together with a repeated movement.

See also ASSEMBLE for the verb form of this sign.

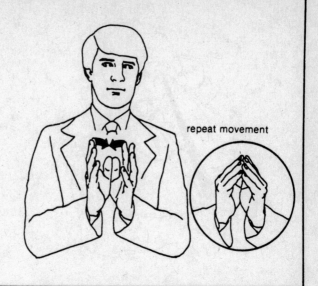

repeat movement

MEMBER, MEMBERSHIP (A)

This is an initialized sign used to refer to a person who belongs to an organization such as a specific congregation.

Formation: Touch the fingertips of the right "m" hand, palm toward the chest, first near the left shoulder and then near the right shoulder.

See also BOARD, BOARD OF DEACONS, and DEACON (B) for other initialized signs formed in a similar manner.

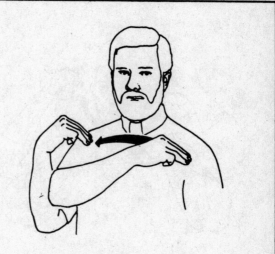

MEMBER (B)

This is a combination of UNITE and the person marker and refers to a person who becomes affiliated with a particular congregation.

Formation: Beginning with both "c" hands apart in front of the chest, palms facing each other, bring them to each other, intersecting the touching thumbtip and index fingertip of each hand with the other. Add the person marker.

See also UNITE for a sign with a related meaning formed in a similar manner.

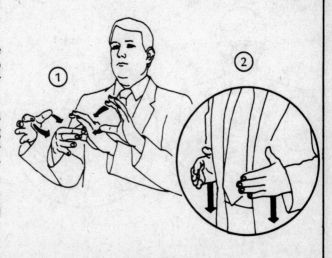

MEMORIAL, REMEMBER, REMEMBRANCE, COMMEMORATE

The hand seems to take a thought from the mind and place it in view for examination.

Formation: Bring the thumb of the "a" right hand from the forehead down to touch the thumbnail of the left "a" hand held in front of the chest, both palms facing down.

MENNONITE

The hands mime tying the bonnet traditionally worn by women who are Mennonites, a religious sect opposed to taking oaths, holding public office, or performing military service.

Formation: Bring both modified "a" hands, palms facing out, from each side of the head down to meet under the chin.

repeat movement

MERCY, PITY, COMPASSION, SYMPATHY (A)

The sign uses the middle finger, the one most frequently used in American Sign Language to denote feelings, and seems to take feeling from one's own heart and then caress the head of an unfortunate person. This is a directional sign that is made toward the person or thing being pitied.

Formation: With the bent middle finger of both "5" hands, palms facing the body, stroke upward in front of the middle of the chest. Then turn the hands, palms facing forward, and stroke outward with a double motion.

MERCY, GOD'S MERCY (B)

This is the directional form of MERCY (A) and symbolizes God's mercy toward mankind.

Formation: With the bent middle fingers of both "5" hands pointing toward the right side of the head, palms facing down, stroke the air toward the head repeatedly.

repeat movement

MESSIAH, MAJESTY

This is an initialized sign that follows the shape of the sash worn by royalty and refers to the Hebrew meaning of Messiah—"the annointed one."

Formation: Touch the fingertips of the right "m" hand, palm left, fist to the left shoulder and then to the right hip.

See also CHRIST, DAVID, KING and LORD (A) for other initialized signs formed in a similar manner.

METHODIST, ZEAL

This sign is a natural gesture used by people who are enthusiastic or eager. It denotes the enthusiasm of the Methodist Revival Movement in the eighteenth century, which led to the establishment of the church based on the teachings of John and Charles Wesley.

Formation: Rub the palms of both hands together with alternating back and forth movements, fingers pointing forward.

Same sign for ENTHUSIASTIC, ANXIOUS, AMBITIOUS, EAGER

alternating movement

MEZUZAH (A)

The fingers inscribe an imaginary mezuzah, the small container, on the doorposts of Jewish homes holding biblical passages written on parchment.

Formation: Move the fingertips of the right "g" hand, palm facing out, downward a short distance in front of the right shoulder.

MEZUZAH (B)

This sign refers to the custom of kissing the mezuzah on the doorpost of a home or other building before entering.

Formation: Pat the fingertips of the right open hand first against the lips and then forward against the open left palm facing the body in front of the chest.

See also JERUSALEM for a sign formed in a similar manner.

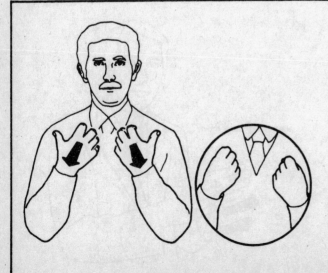

MIGHTY, COURAGE, HEALING, WHOLE (A)

The hands seem to demonstrate health and strength.

Formation: Bring both "5" hands, palms facing body, from each side of the chest near the shoulders deliberately forward while changing into "s" hands.

Same sign for BRAVE, COURAGEOUS, HEALTH, STRENGTH, STRONG, WELL

See also ALMIGHTY and POWER for related signs.

MIGHTY, AUTHORITY, POWERFUL (B)

The hand of this initialized sign follows the shape of a flexed muscle as an indication of God's power to command and exact obedience from all things.

Formation: Move the right "a" hand, palm facing in, from near the left shoulder in an arc to the crook of the left extended arm.

Same sign for ENERGY, STRONG

See also ALMIGHTY and POWER for related signs.

MILLENNIUM

This sign is a combination of ONE, THOUSAND, and YEAR and signifies the belief regarding a thousand-year period of holiness during which Christ is to rule on earth.

Formation: Point the index finger up, palm facing forward. Then tap the fingertips of the right "m" hand into the open palm of the left hand, palms facing. Next with both "s" hands, palms facing in opposite, move the right hand forward and around the left hand, landing on top of the left hand.

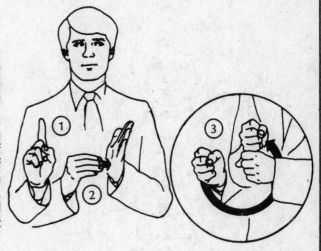

MINISTER

This initialized sign is formed like SERVE and refers to duties and services performed by the clergy.

Formation: Move both "m" hands, palms facing up several inches apart in front of the body, forward with an alternating back and forth movement.

See also SERVE for another sign with a related meaning formed in a similar manner.

alternating movement

repeat movement

MINISTRY

This is an initialized sign with an action similar to that of PREACH.

Formation: Tap the heel of the right "m" hand, palm forward, on the back of the left "s" hand, palm down.

repeat movement

MIRACLE, MARVEL

This sign is a combination of WONDERFUL and WORK and signifies an unexplainable event held to be an act of God or the supernatural.

Formation: Pat the air repeatedly with both "5" hands, palms facing forward near each shoulder. Then tap the heel of the right "s" hand, palm facing down, on the back of the left "s" hand with a double movement.

See also WONDERFUL for an alternate sign for MARVEL.

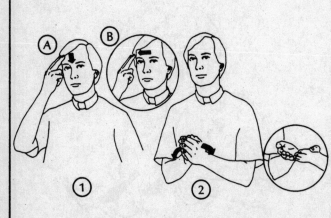

MISSAL

This sign is a combination of CATHOLIC and BOOK and indicates the book containing the prayers and responses necessary for celebrating the Roman Catholic Mass.

Formation: Draw the "u" hand downward in front of the forehead, palm toward the face and fingers pointing up. Then bring the "u" hand, fingers still pointing up, from left to right in front of the forehead. Then starting with both palms touching in front of the chest, fingers pointing forward, move the hands apart at the top, keeping the little fingers together.

MISSION

This is an initialized sign near the heart and indicates that the heart motivates the religious or charitable work done either in foreign countries or in areas without assigned clergy.

Formation: Move the right "m" hand, palm left, in a small circle over the heart.

See also NATURE (B) for an initialized sign formed in a similar manner.

MISSIONARY

This initialized sign is a combination of MISSION and the person marker and refers to a person sent to do religious work in an unchurched area or foreign country.

Formation: Move the right "m" hand, palm left, in a small circle over the heart. Add the person marker.

MITZVAH

This initialized sign is formed like DO and indicates the 613 commandments which, according to tradition, Jews are obligated to observe.

Formation: Move both "m" hands, palms down, back and forth in front of the waist.

See also WORKS for a sign with a related meaning formed in a similar manner.

See also BAR MITZVAH and BAT MITZVAH for signs with related meanings.

repeat movement

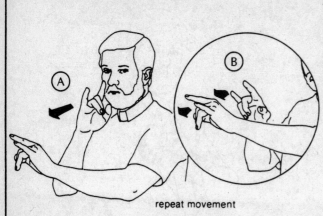

repeat movement

MOCK, SCORN, BETRAY, DECEIVE

The fingers seem to poke fun at someone.

Formation: With the index and little fingers of both hands extended, place the right index fingertip against the side of the nose, palm left, and the left hand lower and forward, palm down, move both hands forward with two deliberate movements.

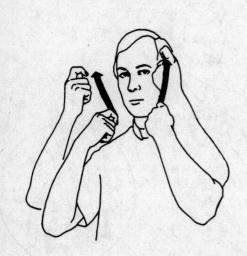

MONK

The hands mime pulling up a hood, which is worn by the members of a religious brotherhood devoted to the disciplines prescribed by their order.

Formation: Move both "a" hands with the knuckles of both index fingers slightly extended, palms facing in, from each side of the chin up toward the top of the head.

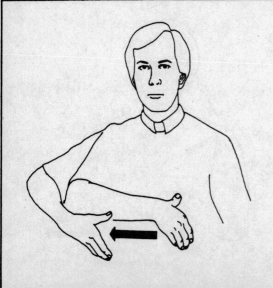

MONSIGNOR

The hand outlines the traditional red sash worn by Monsignors in the Roman Catholic Church.

Formation: Bring the right "c" hand, palm facing body, around the waist from left to right.

MORMON, LATTER-DAY SAINTS (A)

This is an initialized sign used to refer to the church founded by Joseph Smith in 1830 in Fayette, New York.

Formation: Brush the fingertips of the right "m" hand from the right temple downward and slightly outward near the right cheek.

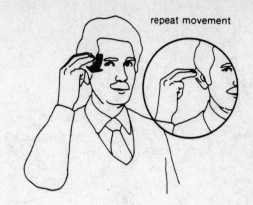

repeat movement

MORMON, LATTER-DAY SAINTS (B)

This is an initialized sign signifying the Church of Jesus Christ of Latter-Day Saints, also known as the Mormon Church.

Formation: Form an L, D, and S with the right hand, palm out, in front of the right side of the chest, moving the hand slightly to the right for each letter.

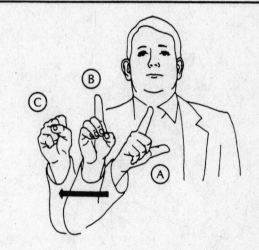

MOSES

This is an initialized sign formed like LAW and refers to the lawgiver who led the Israelites out of Egypt.

Formation: Move the right "m" hand, palm down, first against the fingers and then the base of the open left palm, facing right.

See also COMMANDMENTS, HALACHA (A), LAW (B), and TESTAMENT for other initialized signs formed in a similar manner.

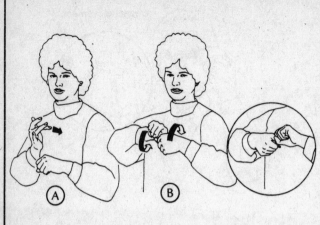

MOURN, GRIEVE, GRIEF

This sign is a combination of FEEL and a twisting gesture that demonstrates a heart being crushed.

Formation: Tap the bent middle finger of the "5" hand, palm toward the body and fingers pointing left, on the center of the chest. Then with the right "s" hand, palm facing forward, over the left "s" hand, palm facing the body, twist the hands, reversing the orientation of the palms.

See also SORROW and SUFFER for signs with similar meaning.

MYSTERY, HIDDEN

This sign is similar to HIDE and denotes the hidden truths revealed through Christ to the elect. The sign is also used to signify any of the fifteen incidents in Christ's life regarded by the Roman Catholic Church as having mystical significance.

Formation: With the back of the "a" thumb touching the lips, palm left, move the hand down and forward under and past the downturned left bent hand.

NATURE (A)

This is an initialized sign used to indicate man's natural state, as opposed to the state of grace.

Formation: Move the fingertips of the right "n" hand, palm down, in a circle over and down on the back of the downturned left open hand.

Note: The left hand may be an "s" hand.

Same sign for NATURALLY, NATION, NATIONAL, OF COURSE

NATURE (B)

This is an initialized sign formed near the heart and refers to the intrinsic characteristics and qualities of a person.

Formation: Move the right "n" hand, palm left, in a small circle over the heart.

See also MISSION for an initialized sign formed in a similar manner.

repeat movement

NAZARETH

This is a combination of an initialized sign and TOWN and is used to designate the town in which Jesus spent his childhood.

Formation: Twist the right "n" hand, palm down, slightly outward near the right shoulder. Then with palms facing and hands held at a slight angle, tap the fingertips together first in front of the left side of the chest and then again in front of the right side of the chest.

See also BETHLEHEM and JERUSALEM (A) for other initialized signs formed in a similar manner.

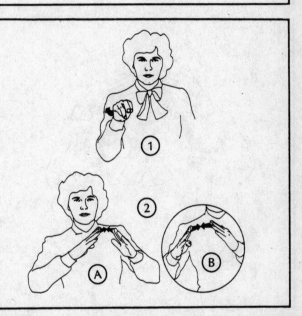

NEW TESTAMENT

This sign is a combination of NEW and TESTAMENT and is used to specify the Gospels, Acts, Epistles, and the Book of Revelation, which together are considered by Christians as forming the record of the new dispensation of the church.

Formation: Sweep the back of the right bent open hand, palm up, upward across the heel of the upturned left hand. Then move the right "t" hand, palm left, across the left open palm, facing forward and fingers pointing up, touching first at the fingers and then at the heel.

See also OLD TESTAMENT for a sign with a related meaning.

NUN, SISTER (A)

This is an initialized sign that follows the outline of the traditional headdress worn by nuns, women belonging to a religious order who have vowed a life of religious service in the Catholic, Orthodox, or Anglican churches.

Formation: Move both "n" hands, palms facing each other, from touching each temple down to touching each shoulder.

See also VEIL for an initialized sign formed in a similar manner.

NUN, SISTER (B)

The hands follow the shape of the traditional headdress worn by nuns.

Formation: Move both open hands, palms facing the head, from on top of each side of the head down to touching each shoulder.

See also VEIL for an initialized sign formed in a similar manner.

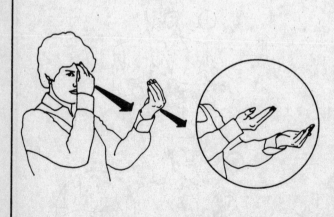

OBEY, OBEDIENCE

The hands indicate putting one's own ideas in obeisance to another's.

Formation: Move both flat "o" hands from the right hand touching the right temple and the left hand somewhat forward, both palms toward face, down simultaneously while opening into bent open hands, palms up, in front of the body.

Note: The hands can begin as "a" hands. The head should bow slightly as the hands move forward.

See also DISOBEY for the sign with the opposite meaning.

OBLIGATION, RESPONSIBILITY, BURDEN, FAULT, BEAR

The hands seem to place a heavy burden on the shoulders.

Formation: With the fingertips of both bent hands on the right shoulder, palms down, drop the shoulder and right side of the body.

See also ACCUSE for a sign with a related meaning.

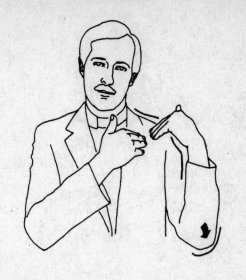

OBTAIN, RECEIVE, GET, ACQUIRE

The hands take something and bring it to oneself.

Formation: Begin with the little-finger side of the right "5" hand perpendicular across the index-finger side of the left "5" hand, palms facing each other. Bring both hands, palms facing down, in to the chest, while drawing the thumbs and fingertips together.

See also CONCEIVE for a directional form of this sign.

OFFERING, OFFER, PRESENT, OBLATION

The hands lay something before another, as in act of worship or thanksgiving to God.

Formation: Bring both upturned hands, fingers angled up and the right hand slightly higher than the left, in a deliberate upward motion.

Same sign for SUGGEST, PROPOSE

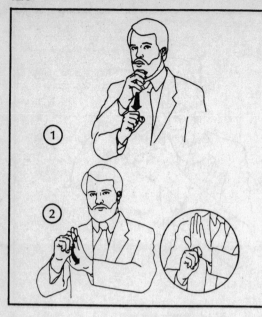

OLD TESTAMENT

This sign is a combination of OLD and TESTAMENT and is used to designate the Pentateuch, the Prophets, and the Hagiographa, which are the foundation of Judaism and which are shared with Christians as the first of two main parts of their Bible.

Formation: Bring the right "c" hand, palm facing left, down from the chin changing into an "s" handshape. Then move the right "t" hand, palm facing left, across the left open palm, facing forward and fingers pointing up, touching first at the fingers and then at the heel.

See also NEW TESTAMENT for a sign with a related meaning.

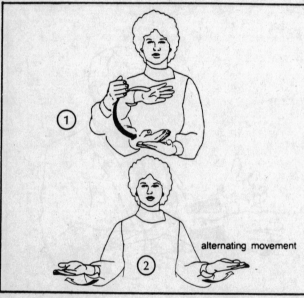

alternating movement

OMNIPRESENT

This sign is a combination of ALL and HERE and signifies God's attribute of being present everywhere.

Formation: With the open right hand, palm facing out, near the left side of the chest, make a large loop to the right, ending palm up in the upturned left palm. Then move both upturned hands back and forth in opposite directions in front of the waist.

OMNISCIENT

This sign is a combination of KNOW, ALL, and THINGS, and refers to the attribute of total knowledge ascribed to God.

Formation: Tap the fingertips of the bent right hand to the right temple, palm facing down. Then with the open right hand, palm facing out near the left shoulder, make a large loop to the right ending palm up in the upturned left palm. Move both upturned curved hands from alongside each other in front of the body outward in an arc apart from each other.

ONLY, SOLE

Shows being the only one of a kind, such as God's characteristics that set him apart from others.

Formation: Beginning with the palm of the right "one" hand facing out, twist the wrist so the palm faces the body.

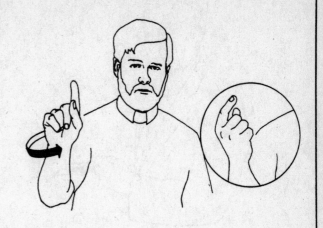

ORDAIN, ORDINATION, HOLY ORDERS

The hands symbolize the act of ordination which, invests a person with priestly or ministerial authority.

Formation: Move the right downturned hand from on top of the head down to on top of the left downturned hand held in front of the body.

See also CONFIRMATION (A) (B) and IN-STALL for signs for related meanings.

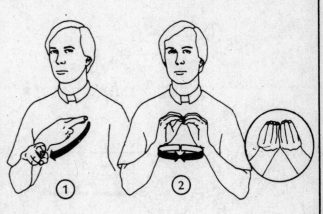

ORDER

This sign is a combination of RELIGIOUS and ORGANIZATION and refers to certain monastic institutions.

Formation: Touch the fingertips of the right "r" hand to the left side of the chest, palm facing the body. Then move the "r" hand smoothly down and outward, ending with the palm facing left and the fingers pointing outward. Beginning with the fingertips of both "o" hands together, palms facing each other, move the hands outward in a circle until the little fingers meet.

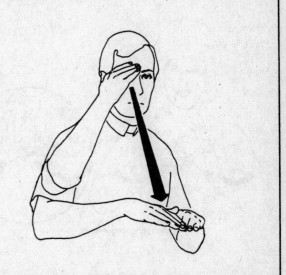

ORTHODOX

This is an initialized sign formed like CLEAN and designates those Jews who adhere to strict traditional practices and beliefs.

Formation: Move the right "o" hand, palm facing down, across the upturned left palm from the base to the fingertips.

See also CONSERVATIVE, DIVINE, HOLY (B), PURE (A), RIGHTEOUS (A), and SAINT for other initialized signs formed in a similar manner.

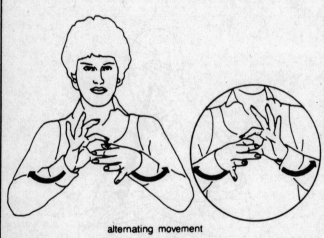

alternating movement

PARABLE, MESSAGE, STORY, TALE (A)

This sign is used to refer to the stories told by Jesus that illustrated moral or religious issues.

Formation: With the thumbtip and index fingertip of each hand touching the other hand, left hand above the right hand, twist the wrists to touch again with the right hand over the left. Repeat several times.

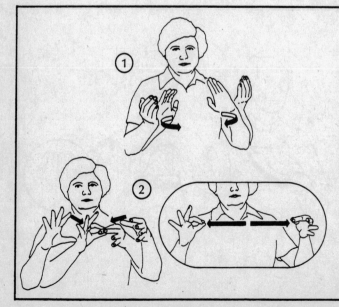

PARABLE (B)

This sign is a combination of COMPARE and SENTENCE and refers to the relationship that Jesus's stories had to everyday life.

Formation: Beginning with both cupped hands held several inches apart in front of the chest, palms facing forward, move them forward in a circle, ending with the palms facing the body. Then bring the thumbtip and index fingertip of each hand to intersect with the other hand, palms facing each other. Pull the "f" hands straight apart.

Note: PARABLE (A) may be substituted for the second part of this sign.

PARISH

This is an initialized sign formed like CHURCH and designates the area and people in a diocese served by a Roman Catholic Church.

Formation: Tap the heel of the right "p" hand, palm facing down, on the top of the downturned left "s" hand.

See also CHURCH, LUTHERAN (B), PETER, SYNAGOGUE, and TEMPLE for other initialized signs formed in a similar manner.

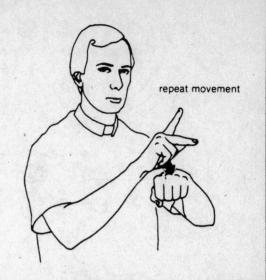

repeat movement

PASSOVER, PESACH (A)

This is an initialized sign in which one hand is passed over the other and represents the angel of the Lord passing over the homes of those with lamb's blood on the doorposts, thus saving the life of the firstborn Jewish boy within.

Formation: Move the right "p" hand, palm down, from in front of the chest forward over the back of the downturned left "s" hand.

PASSOVER, PESACH (B)

This is an initialized sign formed like CRACKER and refers to the matzoth, the unleavened bread eaten at Passover.

Formation: Tap the thumb side of the right "p" hand, palm down, on the elbow of the bent left arm held across the chest.

repeat movement

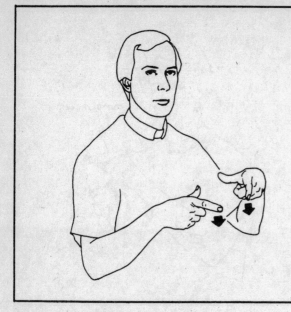

PATEN, PLATE

The fingers encircle the plate, usually made of gold, that is used to hold the Eucharistic bread.

Formation: Tap the curved "l" hands held several inches apart in front of the body, palms facing each other, downward slightly.

repeat movement

PAUL, SAINT PAUL

This is an initialized sign used to refer to Saul of Tarsus whose life and writings are recorded in the Acts of the Apostles and his epistles.

Formation: Tap the middle finger of the right "p" hand, palm toward face, on the right side of the forehead.

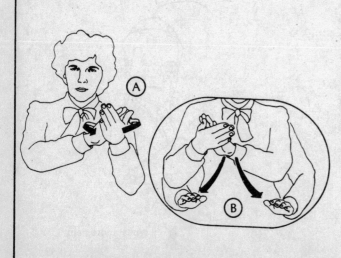

PEACE, SHALOM

The hands move with a quieting motion to indicate a calming serenity over everything.

Formation: Bring both open hands, palms facing angled outward, in a smooth movement from in front of the mouth downward and outward to about shoulder width at the lower-chest level.

131

PENTECOST, WHITSUNDAY, PONTIAS PILATE

This initialized sign indicates the descent of the Holy Spirit in tongues of fire on the heads of the apostles. It is used in the Christian Church for the festival occurring on the seventh Sunday after Easter. It is also used to refer to Pontias Pilate, who was responsible for putting Jesus to death. The context will determine which meaning is intended.

Formation: Tap the middle finger of the right "p" hand, palm down, once in front of the body and then move it to the right and tap it downward again.

See also CHARISMATIC (B) and TONGUE (A)(B) for signs with related meanings.

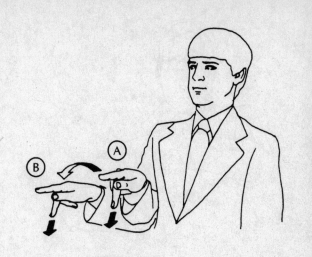

PERSECUTE, PERSECUTION

The hands seem to prod at a person in a repeated harassing manner.

Formation: Beginning with the right "x" hand, palm left, held closer to the body than the left "x" hand, palm right, deliberately push the little-finger side of the right hand across the thumb side of the left hand. Then raise the left hand to repeat the action with the left hand.

Same sign for PROBATION

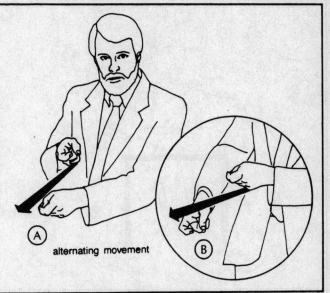

alternating movement

PERSONAL, PERSON

This initialized sign follows the contour of the body.

Formation: Bring both "p" hands, palms facing each other, downward along the body in a parallel movement.

See also LAYPERSON for the plural form of this sign.

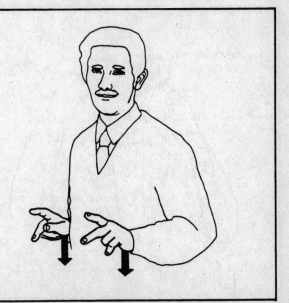

repeat movement

PETER, SAINT PETER, SIMON PETER

This is an initialized sign formed like ROCK and indicates the symbolic name conferred by Christ on Simon, which, translated from the Greek, means "rock."

Formation: Tap the middle finger of the right "p" hand, palm down, on the back of the downturned left "s" hand.

See also CHURCH, LUTHERAN (B), PARISH, SYNAGOGUE, and TEMPLE for other initialized signs formed in a similar manner.

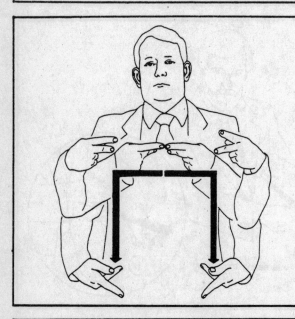

PHARISEE

This is an initialized sign in which the hands follow the form of the breastplate worn by the members of the ancient Jewish sect that emphasized strict interpretation and observance of the Mosaic law.

Formation: Beginning with the middle finger of both "p" hands touching the center of the chest, palms toward the body, bring the hands straight out to the sides of the chest and then straight down to each side of the waist, palms facing up.

See also PRIEST for a sign formed in a similar manner.

repeat movement

PONDER, WONDER, MEDITATE

The action of the hands show a deep, thoughtful consideration of a matter.

Formation: Move the extended index fingers of both hands in small circles pointing at each temple, palms facing back.

Note: The sign may be made with only one hand.

Same sign for CONTEMPLATE, CONSIDER

See also MEDITATE for an initialized alternate sign.

POOR, POVERTY

The hand show the worn-out elbows on the clothes of poor people.

Formation: Place the thumb and fingertips of the right bent "5" hand, palm facing up, on the left elbow. Bring the right hand downward with a double motion, closing the fingertips and thumb each time.

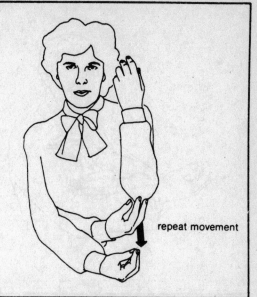

repeat movement

POPE, PAPAL, PONTIFF

The hands follow the shape of the two-tiered miter traditionally worn by the Pope, the head of the Roman Catholic Church who acts as the vicar of Christ on earth.

Formation: Move both open hands from each side of the head, palms facing each other, upward moving in and out in a double arc.

See also BISHOP (B) for a sign formed in a similar manner.

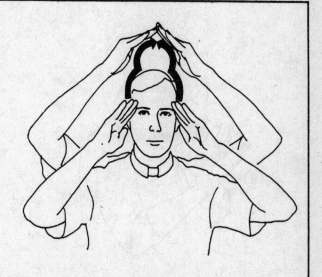

POWER, POWERFUL, MIGHT, STRENGTH, STRONG, ALMIGHTY (A)

This sign is a natural gesture of tightening the biceps by clenching the fists to show strength.

Formation: Move both "s" hands, palms facing the body, from in front of the right side of the chest outward toward the right with force.

See also ALMIGHTY and MIGHTY for alternate signs.

POWER, POWERFUL, MIGHT, STRENGTH, STRONG (B)

The hand outlines a large flexed biceps, symbolizing physical strength.

Formation: Bring the curved "b" right hand from the top of the left shoulder, right index finger touching shoulder and palm down, in an arc down turning the right hand over until the little-finger side, palm up, touches the crook of the extended bent left arm.

Note: The right extended index finger may be used instead of the "b" hand.

See also ALMIGHTY and MIGHTY for alternate signs.

PRAISE, MAGNIFY, HOSANNA (A)

The hands mime applauding to extol or exalt God.

Formation: Start with the right extended index finger at the lips, palm left. Then pat the downturned right open hand on the palm of the upturned left open hand, which is held in front of the face.

Same sign for ACCLAIM, APPLAUD, CLAP, COMMEND, OVATION

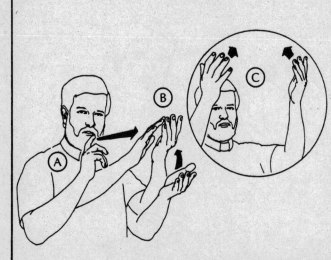

PRAISE, MAGNIFY, HOSANNA (B)

This sign is a combination of the hands miming applause and OFFER.

Formation: Start with the right extended index finger at the lips, palm left. Then pat the downturned right open hand on the palm of the upturned left open hand, which is held in front of the face. Then raise both open hands upward with the palms angled up.

Same sign for ACCLAIM, APPLAUD

PRAY, PRAYER, AMEN, LITANY INTERCESSION, COLLECT, SUPPLICATION, PETITION

The hands mime a natural pleading motion to indicate any communion with God, such as confession, petition, or praise.

Formation: With both open hands, palms against each other and fingers angled up and forward, move hands inward and downward slightly in a double motion.

See also WORSHIP for an alternate sign for AMEN.

PREACH, SERMON, HOMILY, ENLIGHTEN

This sign is formed like LECTURE and refers to a speech that gives religious or moral instruction.

Formation: Move the right "f" hand, palm forward, at the side of the face forward with several small jerky motions.

See also EVANGELISM (B) for a sign formed in a similar manner.

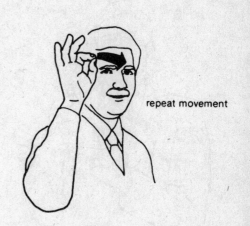

repeat movement

PREACHER, MINISTER, PASTOR

This sign is a combination of PREACH plus the person marker and designates Protestant clergy.

Formation: Move the right "f" hand, palm forward, at the side of the face forward with several small jerky motions. Add the person marker.

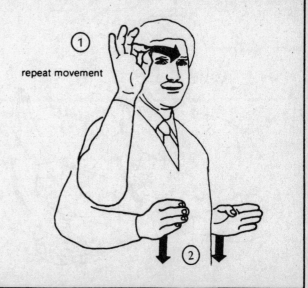

repeat movement

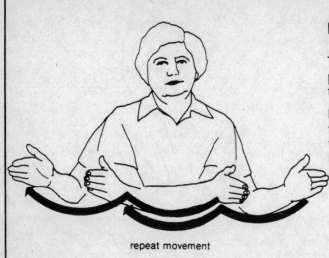

repeat movement

PREPARE, PREPARATION

The hands seem to be clearing different paths and symbolize mankind's preparation for eternal life.

Formation: Move both open hands, palms facing each other several inches apart and fingers pointing forward, from left to right in front of the waist in several arcs.

repeat movement

PRESBYTERIAN

This is an initialized sign used to designate various Protestant churches, which are traditionally Calvinist in doctrine and governed by presbyters and elders.

Formation: Tap the middle finger of the right "p" hand, palm left, into the center of the left palm, angled up and fingers pointing forward.

PRESENCE, APPEARANCE, APPEAR BEFORE, COME BEFORE

The hands represent a person coming before another person. If referring to the presence of God, the left hand is held somewhat higher than the right, indicating God's elevated position. This is a directional sign.

Formation: Bring both slightly curved hands, palms facing each other and fingertips pointing up, from in front of waist upward in an arc toward each other, stopping a few inches apart.

Same sign for FACE, CONFRONT

See also APPEAR for the sign to use for a sudden appearance.

PRESERVE (A)

This is an initialized sign in which the hands symbolize eyes watching in all directions to keep something safe.

Formation: With the little-finger side of the right "k" hand, palm left, on the index-finger side of the left "k" hand, palm right, move them in a large clockwise flat circle in front of the waist.

Same sign for TAKE CARE OF, KEEP

repeat movement

PRESERVE (B)

This sign is used to refer to long-term caring for of something and refers to God's care over his children.

Formation: With the right "v" fingers on the back of the left "s" hand, both palms facing in, move the hands toward the chest.

Same sign for STORE, KEEP, SAVE

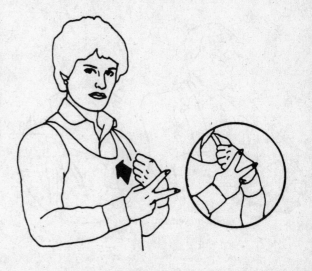

PRIEST (A)

This sign is formed like PHARISEE and designates the ancient priests of the Scriptures.

Formation: Beginning with both extended index fingers touching the center of the chest, palms toward the body, bring the hands straight out to the sides of the chest and then straight down to each side of the waist, palms facing up.

See also PHARISEE for a sign formed in a similar manner.

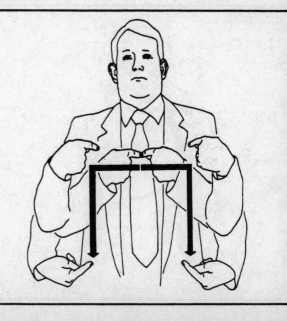

PRIEST, FATHER (B)

The fingers follow the shape of the clerical collar worn by those members of the clergy in the Roman Catholic, Episcopal, and some other churches who have the authority to pronounce absolution and administer the Sacraments.

Formation: Drag the fingertips of the right "g" hand from the left side of the neck, palm facing the body, around the neck to the right.

Note: The sign may be formed with both hands beginning in the middle of the neck, moving apart from each other around the neck.

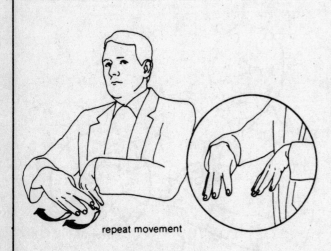

repeat movement

PROCESSION, PARADE, MARCH

The hands represent the feet of marchers moving forward in an orderly and formal manner.

Formation: With the fingers of both "4" hands pointing down, palms toward waist, right hand in front of the left, flip the fingers of both hands forward from the wrists several times.

PROOF, EVIDENCE

The hand takes something that is known and lays it out for examination to verify its truth or existence.

Formation: Bring the extended right index finger, palm left, from the right side of face near the mouth forward and down while changing to an open hand, landing with the back of the upturned right hand on the upturned left palm.

Note: The right hand may begin as an open hand, palm facing back, on the right cheek.

See also WITNESS (A) for a sign with a related meaning formed in a similar manner.

PROPHECY, FORETELL, PREDICT, PREDICTION

This sign is a combination of SEE and LOOK and refers to the inspired revelations of messianic prophets.

Formation: The fingertips of the right "v" hand move from pointing at each eye downward and forward under the left flat hand held in front of the chest, both palms facing down.

See also VISION (B) for a sign with a related meaning formed in a similar manner.

PROPHET

This sign is a combination of PROPHECY and the person marker and refers to those persons who, through divine inspiration, predict the future.

Formation: The fingertips of the right "v" hand move from pointing at each eye downward and forward under the left flat hand held in front of the chest, palms facing down. Add the person marker.

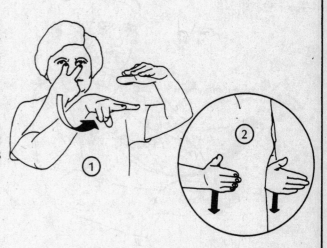

PROTECT, DEFEND, GUARD

The hands are held up as a shield to protect the body.

Formation: With both "s" hands crossed at the wrists in front of the chest, right palm facing left and left palm facing right, move both hands forward with a double motion.

repeat movement

repeat movement

PROTESTANT

The fingers represent bended knees. The sign is used to refer to a Christian belonging to any sect descending from those that seceded from the Catholic Church at the time of the Reformation.

Formation: Knock the knuckles of the bent right "v" fingers, palm facing the body, in the upturned left palm with a double motion.

See also GENUFLECT and KNEEL for signs with related meanings formed in a similar manner.

repeat movement

PSALM, POEM, POETRY

This is an initialized sign formed like SONG and indicates any of the hymns collected in the Old Testament book of Psalms.

Formation: Swing the right "p" hand, palm toward the body, back and forth in a large arc across the top of the extended left arm.

See also CANTOR and HYMN for other signs with related meanings formed in a similar manner.

PUNISH, PUNISHMENT, PENALTY, DISCIPLINE

The hand mimes a punishing movement.

Formation: Strike the extended right index finger, palm down and finger pointing left, downward with a deliberate movement on the elbow of the raised bent left arm.

PURE, PURITY (A)

This is an initialized sign formed like CLEAN and refers to the state of being sinless and perfect.

Formation: Drag the middle fingertip of the right "p" hand, palm down, across the upturned left palm from its base to off the fingertips.

Same sign for CHASTITY

See also CONSERVATIVE, DIVINE, HOLY (B), ORTHODOX, RIGHTEOUS (A), and SAINT (A) for other initialized signs formed in a similar manner.

PURE, PURITY (B)

This initialized sign is a combination of "p" and CLEAN and refers to something that is without defilement.

Formation: Form a "p" with the right hand, palm down, near the base of the upturned left palm. Change to a flat downturned right hand and wipe its palm across the left palm from its base to off the fingertips, keeping the fingers perpendicular to each other.

See also HOLY (A)(C) and SANCTIFY (A) for other initialized signs formed in a similar manner.

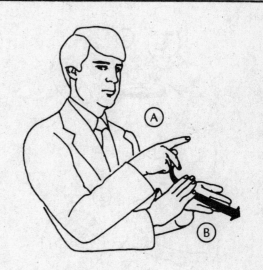

PURGATORY, INDULGENCE

This initialized sign is formed like COIN and refers to the former practice of selling indulgences in the sixteenth century to expiate the sins of souls in purgatory who have died in grace.

Formation: Move the middle finger of the right "p" hand, palm down, in a small circle in the upturned left open palm.

repeat movement

repeat movement

PURIM

The fingers form a mask that represents the Jewish holiday celebrating the deliverance of the Jews from massacre by Haman.

Formation: Starting with the index and middle fingers of both "3" hands touching above and below each eye, palms facing back, pull them outward from the head while repeatedly opening and closing the fingers.

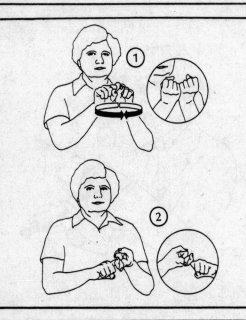

QUAKER, SOCIETY OF FRIENDS, FRIENDS (A)

This sign is a combination of SOCIETY and FRIENDS and signifies the preferred name of this religious sect founded by George Fox in 1650 in England which rejects ritual, formal sacraments, a formal creed, a priesthood, and violence.

Formation: Move both "s" hands, palms facing forward, from touching in front of the chest in a circle outward until the little fingers meet, palms facing the body. Then hook the right bent index finger, palm facing down, over the upturned left bent index finger. Repeat the action in reverse.

See also FRIEND for an alternate sign.

alternating movement

QUAKER, SOCIETY OF FRIENDS, FRIENDS (B)

The hands mime twiddling thumbs to indicate the reputed patience of members of the Quaker Church as they await the Holy Spirit. The name Quaker is not used by members of the church, founded by George Fox, who admonished the members "to tremble at the Word of the Lord."

Formation: Interwine the fingers of both hands with each other, palms facing each other. Revolve the thumbs around each other in a repeated motion.

RABBI

The hands of this initialized sign indicate the location of the Tallith, the prayer shawl worn by the ordained spiritual leader of a Jewish congregation.

Formation: Draw the fingertips of both "r" hands from either shoulder straight down either side of the chest.

See also BROTHER and TALLITH for signs formed in a similar manner.

RECONCILIATION, RECONCILE, COVENANT, ATONE, ATONEMENT (A)

This is a directional sign made like UNITY and indicates Christ's role in uniting God with man.

Formation: With the thumbtip and index fingertip of each hand touching and intersecting with the other hand, the right hand held above the left hand near the right shoulder, palms facing, move the hands upward and downward with a repeated motion.

See also COMMUNION OF SAINTS and UNITY for signs formed in a similar manner.

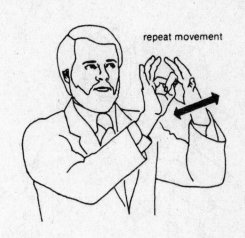

repeat movement

RECONCILIATION, RECONCILE (B)

The hands seem to bring two things together and symbolize God's relationship with man because of Christ's redemptive work.

Formation: Beginning with both cupped hands, palms up the fingers pointing toward each other, in front of each side of the body, bring them together in front of the waist.

Same sign for INTRODUCE, INTRODUCTION.

RECONSTRUCTIONISM

This sign is a combination of RE- and BUILD and signifies a religious movement in the United States that developed out of the Conservative branch of Judaism.

Formation: Form an "r" and "e" with the right hand near the right shoulder. Then with the fingertips of both bent hands overlapping slightly, alternate moving the right and left hands over each other, moving the hands upward each time.

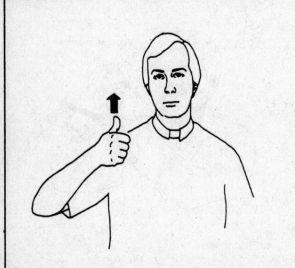

RECTOR, CHIEF, SUPREME

This is the sign for CHIEF and indicates a Roman Catholic priest appointed the spiritual head of a church or seminary.

Formation: Bring the right "a" hand with an extended thumb upward near the right shoulder, palm facing the body.

See also EXALT for a sign with a related meaning.

REDEEM, REDEMPTION

This initialized sign shows the hands breaking free from bondage and refers to the freedom from sin given through Christ's redemptive work.

Formation: Bring both "r" hands, wrists crossed in front of the chest and palms facing in, outward by twisting the wrists away from each other, ending with the palms facing forward near each shoulder.

See also DELIVER, REFORMED, and SALVATION for initialized signs with a related meaning formed in a similar manner.

REDEEMER

This sign is a combination of REDEEM and the person marker refers to Christ's role in redeeming mankind from a state of sinfulness.

Formation: Bring both "r" hands, wrists crossed in front of the chest and palms facing in, outward by twisting the wrists away from each other, ending with the palms facing forward near each shoulder. Add the person marker.

See also SAVIOR for a sign formed in a similar manner.

REFORMED, REFORM JUDAISM

This initialized sign shows the hands breaking free from bondage and refers to the branch of Judaism introduced in the nineteenth century that does not require strict observance of traditional law.

Formation: Beginning with the fingers of both "r" hands pointing up on each side of the chest, palms facing in, bring both hands outward by twisting the wrists away from each other, ending with the palms facing forward near each shoulder.

See also DELIVER, REDEEM, and SALVATION for initialized signs formed in a similar manner.

REJECT, REJECTED, EXCOMMUNICATION (A)

The hand brushes away a rejected object and signifies dismissing someone from participation in the religious community.

Formation: Brush the little-finger side of the right open hand, palm left, from the heel of the upturned left hand across the palm and off the left fingertips upward in an arc by twisting the wrist.

REJECT, REJECTED, EXCOMMUNICATION (B)

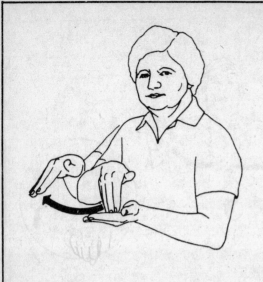

The fingertips brush away an unwanted object or person and refers to cutting a person off from church rites as directed by ecclesiastical authority.

Formation: Brush the fingertips of the right open hand, palm toward the body, from the heel of the upturned left hand across the palm and off the left fingertips with a flick of the wrist.

REJOICE, JOY

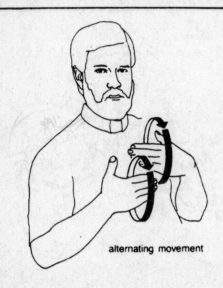

alternating movement

The hands have an upward movement that indicates bringing up happiness from within.

Formation: Bring the flat palm of each hand against the chest with circular outward alternating movements.

Same sign for DELIGHT, GLAD, HAPPY, HAPPINESS, MERRY

See also REVIVAL for an initialized sign with a related meaning formed in a similar manner.

RELIGION, RELIGIOUS

This is an initialized sign that connates an inward faith from the heart as well as outward sincere observance of rituals.

Formation: Touch the fingertips of the right "r" hand to the left side of the chest, palm facing the body. Then move the "r" hand smoothly down and forward ending with the palm facing down and the fingers pointing forward.

Note: The "r" hand may begin on the right side of the chest instead of the left.

See also THEOLOGY (A)(B) for a sign formed in a similar manner and FRUM for the sign that is used for RELIGIOUS when indicating strict Jewish observance.

RENOUNCE, SUBMIT, SURRENDER, SUBMISSION

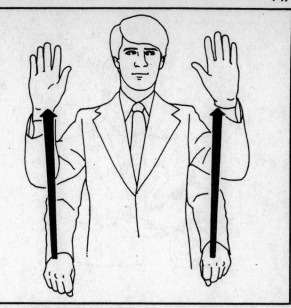

The hands demonstrate a natural gesture of surrender and symbolize a pledge to turn away from sin and the devil's power.

Formation: Beginning with both "s" hands near each side of the waist, bring the hands up abruptly changing to "5" hands, palms forward, above each shoulder.

Same sign for GIVE UP, RELINQUISH

REPENT, REPENTANCE

This initialized sign is formed like CHANGE and indicates a repentant person's regret for past behavior and intent to abjure future sins.

Formation: With the heels of both "r" hands together at angles, the back of the right hand near the chest, twist the wrists in opposite directions, ending with the hands in reverse positions.

See also CONVERT, INTERPRET, and TRANSLATE for other signs formed in a similar manner.

RESPECT, REVERE, REVERENT

This initialized sign is formed like GOD and signifies a deep respect for God.

Formation: Move both "r" hands from above the head, palms facing each other and fingers pointing up, in a slight arc toward the face and down to the chest.

Note: The head is often bowed as the hands come down. This sign may be made with only the right hand.

See also GOD (A)(B) and HONOR for other signs formed in a similar manner.

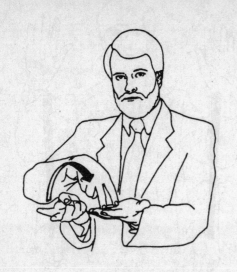

RESURRECTION, ARISE

The fingers demonstrate getting on one's feet and refers to the rising of Christ after the Crucifixion and of the dead at the Last Judgment.

Formation: Beginning with the right "v" hand, palm up, beside the left upturned hand, raise the right hand up in an arc ending with the fingertips of the right "v" hand pointing down on the left palm.

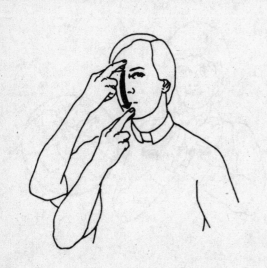

RETREAT

This initialized sign signifies the period of seclusion used for discussing religious practices or issues.

Formation: Move the right "r" hand, palm toward face, from touching the forehead to touching the chin.

Note: As a variation of this sign, the hand may change to a "t" hand at the chin·

REVEAL, REVELATION, EXAMPLE, MANIFEST, MANIFESTATION

The hand brings out something into view for examination. This is a directional sign.

Formation: Touch the extended right index finger into the open left hand, palms facing each other. Move both hands forward a short distance.

Note: The left palm may face forward with the fingers pointing either up or down as a variation of this sign.

Same sign for SHOW, REPRESENT, DEMONSTRATE, EXPRESS

See also SYMBOL and WITNESS (B) for initialized signs formed in a similar manner.

REVIVAL

This is an initialized sign formed like RE-JOICE and signifies the reawakening of faith that frequently occurs ar religious revivals.

Formation: Alternately strike the chest with the fingertips of both "r" hands, palms toward body, with an upward circular motion.

See also REJOICE for a sign with a related meaning formed in a similar manner.

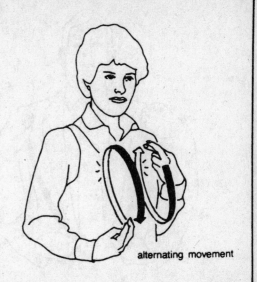

alternating movement

RIGHTEOUS, RIGHTEOUSNESS (A)

This initialized sign is formed like CLEAN and refers to the righteous being cleansed through Christ's redemptive power.

Formation: Push the fingertips of the right "r" hand across the upturned left palm from its base top off the fingertips, palms facing each other.

See also CONSERVATIVE, DIVINE, HOLY (B), ORTHODOX, PURE (A), and SAINT (A) for other initialized signs formed in a similar manner.

RIGHTEOUS, RIGHTEOUSNESS (B)

This sign is formed like ALL RIGHT and refers to those people who have been declared right with God.

Formation: Slide the little-finger side of the right open hand, palm left, across the palm of the upturned left hand from the heel to off the fingertips.

ROBE

The hands show the flow of the garment worn by church officials.

Formation: Bring both hands, thumbs touching the fingertips, from on each shoulder, palms facing the body, down to the waist, ending with the palms facing up.

See also VESTMENTS for a related sign.

ROMAN, ROME, LATIN

This initialized sign follows the shape of a Roman nose and refers to the location of the headquarters of the Roman Catholic Church in Italy.

Formation: Move the right "r" hand, palm facing in, from the center of the forehead to the bridge of the nose.

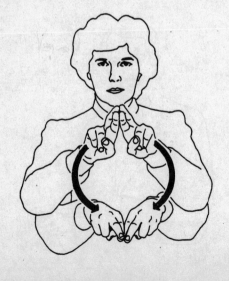

ROSARY

The fingers of this initialized sign follow the shape of the beads on which prayers of devotion are counted to the Virgin Mary.

Formation: Move both "r" hands from the fingers touching and pointing up in front of the chest, palms facing forward, in an arc apart from each other and downward, ending with the "r" fingers touching in front of the waist, palms down.

ROSH HASHANAH, NEW YEAR

This sign is a combination of NEW and YEAR and refers to the Jewish New Year, a solemn occasion celebrated in late September or early October.

Formation: Bring the right palm upward on the chest. Sweep the back of the right bent open hand, palm up, upward across the heel of the upturned left hand. Then with both "s" hands in front of the body, palms facing in and the right hand over the left, move the right hand forward and around left hand, landing on top of the left hand.

RULE, DIRECT, REIGN

The fingers seem to hold the reins of a horse to control it. The sign refers to God's control over the lives of mankind.

Formation: Move both "x" hands, palms facing each other, in alternating movements in and out several inches apart in front of the waist.

Same sign for GOVERN, CONTROL, CONDUCT, MANAGE, OPERATE

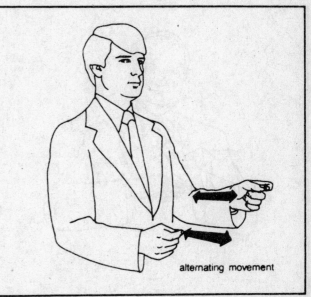

alternating movement

SABBATH (A)

This sign is a combination of REST and DAY and refers to the last day of the week, observed by Jews and some Christian sects as a day of rest and worship.

Formation: Lay the palm of each open hand near the opposite shoulder, crossing the arms on the chest at the wrists. Then place the elbow of the bent right arm, hand held straight up, palm left, on the downturned left hand. Move the extended right index finger downward toward the left elbow, keeping the right elbow in place.

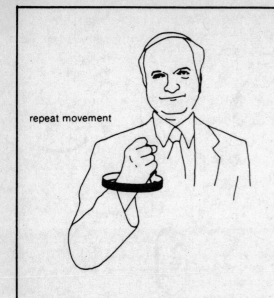

SABBATH, SATURDAY, SHABBAT (B)

This is the sign for SATURDAY, the seventh day of the week designated by some religions as a day of rest and worship.

Formation: Move the right "s" hand, palm facing the body, in a small circle in front of the right side of the chest.

repeat movement

SABBATH, SHABBAT (C)

The hand represents the sun going down behind the horizon and signifies the beginning of the Jewish sabbath on Friday at sundown.

Formation: Bring the right "f" hand, palm facing left, down in front of the chest behind the downturned open left hand held in front of the chest.

SABBATH, SUNDAY (D)

The sign is formed like WONDERFUL and is used to designate the first day of the week, observed by most Christian churches as a day of rest.

Formation: Move both open hands, palms facing forward in front of each shoulder, in circular motions upward and outward from each other.

repeat movement

SACRAMENT

This initialized sign is made in the form of a cross and designates those rites mediating grace that are considered to have been instituted by Christ.

Formation: Move the right "s" hand, palm facing forward, from above the right shoulder downward. Then move the right "s" hand from in front of the right shoulder outward to the right.

See also CROSS and EUCHARIST for other signs formed in a similar manner.

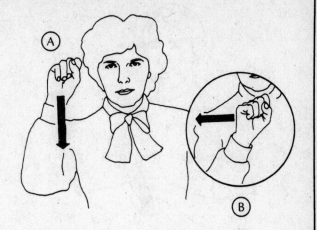

SACRIFICE

This sign is formed like OFFER and indicates that a sacrifice is the offering of something of value to God. This is a directional sign toward God.

Formation: Hold both upturned "s" hands apart in front of the waist. Then bring both hands upward to above the head while opening them into "5" hands, palms facing up.

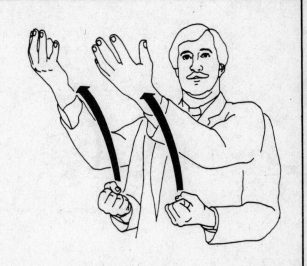

SACRILEGIOUS

This is a directional sign toward God formed like DON'T CARE and indicates an irreverence toward anything sacred.

Formation: Move the extended index finger, palm toward face, outward and upward from the nose, ending with the finger pointing up and the palm facing forward above the right side of the head.

SAINT (A)

This is an initialized sign formed like HOLY and indicates a baptized believer in Christ or, in the Catholic Church, a person who has been canonized and is therefore entitled to public veneration.

Formation: Drag the palm side of the right "s" hand across the upturned left palm from its base to the fingertips and outward.

See also CONSERVATIVE, DIVINE, HOLY (B), ORTHODOX, PURE, RIGHTEOUS (A), SAINT, and SANCTIFY for other initialized signs formed in a similar manner.

SAINT (B)

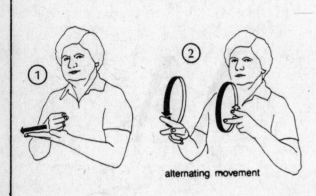

alternating movement

This sign is a combination of HOLY and PEOPLE and signifies all believers on earth and those who have died and gone to heaven.

Formation: Move the little-finger side of the right "h" hand across the upturned open left palm from its base to off the fingertips keeping the fingers perpendicular to each other. Then using both "p" hands, circle them forward with alternating movements.

SALVATION, SAVE, DELIVER

The hands of this initialized sign seem to break free of bondage and symbolize the deliverance of man's soul through Christ's redemption from the penalty of sin.

Formation: Bring both "s" hands, wrists crossed in front of the chest and palms facing in, outward by twisting the wrists away from each other, ending with the palms facing forward near each shoulder.

Same sign for RESCUE, SAFE

See also DELIVER, REDEEM and REFORMED for initialized signs with a similar meaning formed in a similar manner.

SANCTIFY, SANCTIFICATION (A)

This is an initialized sign formed like CLEAN and signifies the act of making something clear or holy.

Formation: Form a right "s" hand, palm facing the body, with the little finger side on the base of the upturned left hand. Change to a flat right hand and wipe the right palm across the left palm from its base to off the fingertips keeping the fingers perpendicular to each other.

See also HOLY (A) and PURE (B) for other initialized signs formed in a similar manner.

SANCTIFY, SANCTIFICATION, CONSECRATE, CONSECRATION (B)

This sign is a combination of MAKE and HOLY and signifies the practice of setting something aside as holy.

Formation: With the right "s" hand on top of the left "s" hand, palms facing each other, twist the wrists in opposite directions repeatedly, touching the hands together with each twist. Then form an "h" with the right hand near the base of the upturned left palm. Change to a flat right hand and wipe the palm of the right hand across the left palm.

See also HOLY (A) and PURE (B) for other initialized signs formed in a similar manner.

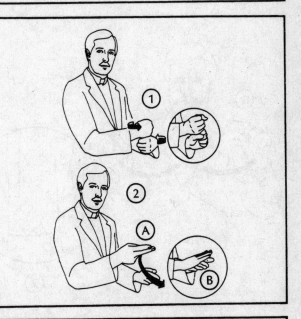

SANCTUARY, SACRISTY, VESTRY, SHRINE

This sign is a combination of HOLY and PLACE and refers to a sacred place, such as a church, temple, or mosque, or a most holy place within that place.

Formation: Make a circle with the right "h" hand near the base of the upturned left palm. Change to a flat right hand and wipe the palm of the right hand across the left palm from its base to off the fingertips keeping the fingers perpendicular to each other. Then with the middle fingers of both "p" hands touching, palms facing up, bring the hands outward in a circle toward the body, ending by touching the middle fingers close to the lower chest.

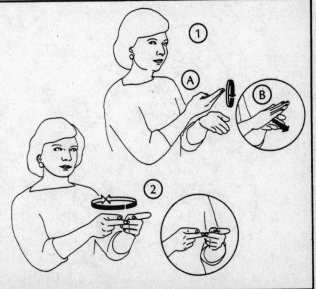

SATISFACTION, SATISFY

Then hands demonstrate controlling inner feeling and refers to reparation in the form of penance for sin.

Formation: Bring both downturned flat hands, right hand above the left, against the chest.

SAVIOR

This is a combination of SAVE and the person marker and designates Christ's role in rescuing mankind from their sins.

Formation: Bring both "s" hands, wrists crossed in front of the chest and palms facing in, outward by twisting the wrists away from each other, ending with the palms facing forward near each shoulder. Add the person marker.

See also REDEEMER for a sign with a related meaning formed in a similar manner.

SCRIPTURE, WRITE, WRITINGS

The hand mimes writing and signifies the sacred writings contained in the Holy Scriptures.

Formation: Move the extended right thumb and index finger together, palm facing down, across the palm of the upturned left open palm.

SEDER

This sign is a combination of PASSOVER and FEAST and represents the feast celebrated on the first two days of Passover, which commemorate the Exodus of the Israelites from Egypt.

Formation: Move the right "p" hand, palm down, from in front of the chest forward over the back of the downturned left "s" hand. Then with the thumb and fingertips of each hand together, palms facing in, bring the fingertips of each hand to the mouth with alternating movements.

Note: The illustration shows PASSOVER (A) for the first position of the sign. However, PASSOVER (B) may be used, if preferred.

SEMINARY

This is an initialized sign formed like COLLEGE and indicates a theological school of higher education for the training of priests, ministers, or rabbis.

Formation: Bring the downturned right "s" hand from on the upturned left palm in a counterclockwise circular motion upward in front of the chest.

See also YESHIVA (A) for another initialized sign formed in a similar manner.

SERVANT

This sign is a combination of SERVE and the person marker and designates someone who expresses submission to God.

Formation: Move both open hands, palms up several inches apart in front of the chest, forward with an alternating back and forth movement. Add the person marker.

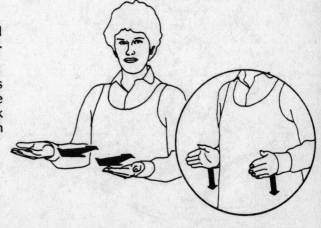

SERVE, SERVICE, MINISTER

The hands seem to carry a tray while serving representing performing acts of benefit to others as evidence of love of God.

Formation: Move both open hands, palms up several inches apart in front of the body, forward with an alternating back and forth movement.

See also MINISTER for an initialized sign with a related meaning formed in a similar manner.

SEVENTH-DAY ADVENTIST (A)

This initialized sign refers to the Adventist Church, which believes that Christ's second coming and the end of the world are near and that the Sabbath should be observed on Saturday.

Formation: Form the letters S, D, and A in front of the right shoulder, palm facing out, moving slightly to the right with each letter.

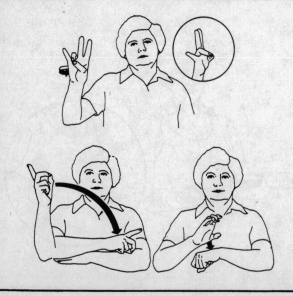

SEVENTH-DAY ADVENTIST (B)

This sign is a combination of SEVENTH, DAY, and CHURCH and refers to members of the Adventist sect that observes its Sabbath on Saturday.

Formation: Form a "7" right hand, palm facing forward, near the right shoulder, then twist the palm sharply toward the head. Next place the elbow of the bent right arm, hand held straight up, palm left, on the downturned left arm. Move the extended right index finger downward toward the left elbow keeping the right elbow in place. Then tap the thumb side of the right "c" hand on the back of the downturned "s" hand.

SHAVUOTH, FEAST OF WEEKS

The sign is the same as SEVEN WEEKS and refers to the Jewish holiday that commemorates the revelation of the Law on Mount Sinai and the celebration of the wheat festival in ancient times.

Formation: Move the fingertips of the right "7" hand, palm down, across the upturned left palm from its base to the fingertips.

SHEEP, LAMB

The hands mime the shearing of wool from sheep.

Formation: With the left upturned hand extended, repeatedly sweep the right "k" hand, palm up, up the inside of the left arm.

Note: For LAMB the sign SMALL may be added before or after SHEEP.

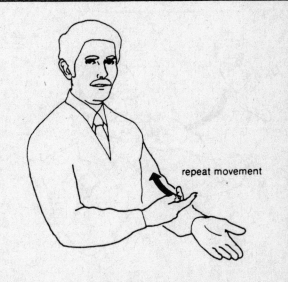

repeat movement

SHEPHERD

This sign is a combination of SHEEP, SUPERVISE, and the person marker and indicates a person who herds, guards, and cares for sheep.

Formation: With the left upturned hand extended, repeatedly sweep the right "k" hand, palm up, up the inside of the left arm. Then with the little-finger side of the right "k" hand, palm left, touching the index-finger side of the left "k" hand, palm right, move both hands in a counterclockwise circle. Add the person marker.

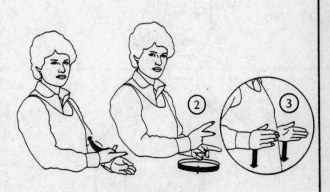

repeat movement

SHIVAH, SITTING SHIVAH

This sign is a combination of SIT and MOURN and signifies the seven-day period of formal mourning observed after the death of a close Jewish relative.

Formation: Lay the fingers of the right "h" hand across the fingers of the left "h" hand, both palms facing down. Then with the right "s" hand, palm facing forward, over the left "s" hand, palm facing the body, twist the hands, reversing the orientation of the palms.

SHOFAR

The hands follow the shape of the trumpet made of a ram's horn that is sounded in the synagogue at Rosh Hashanah and Yom Kippur.

Formation: Beginning with both tight "c" hands in front of the mouth, palms facing each other and left hand closer to the mouth than the right, move the right hand outward and upward in a large arc.

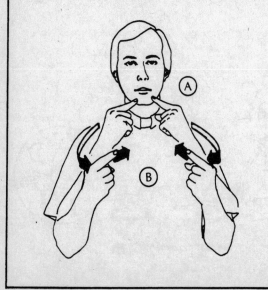

SIN, TRESPASS, TRANSGRESSION, INIQUITY, OFFENSE (A)

This sign is a combination of TELL and HURT and symbolizes how the sin of lying hurts others.

Formation: Move both extended index fingers from pointing to each side of the mouth, palms facing the body, down in an outward arc to jabbing at each other in front of the chest.

SIN, TRESPASS, TRANSGRESSION, INIQUITY, OFFENSE (B)

The fingers move in opposition to each other, indicating the way that sin violates religious or moral laws.

Formation: Beginning with both extended index fingers pointing toward each other in front of the body, palms facing in, move them in repeated circular motions toward and away from each other.

repeat movement

SIN, TRESPASS, TRANSGRESSION, INIQUITY, OFFENSE (C)

The hands seem to churn up an inner turmoil caused by a deliberate violation of God's laws.

Formation: With both "x" hands make simultaneous circles by moving the hands upward and outward, palms facing up in front of each side of the waist.

repeat movement

SIN, TRESPASS, TRANSGRESSION, INIQUITY, OFFENSE (D)

This sign is a combination of WRONG and DO, indicating that sin is doing something that violates moral or religious laws.

Formation: Tap the chin with the middle fingers of the right "y" hand several times, palm facing body. Then swing both downturned "c" hands back and forth in opposite directions to and from each other several times in front of the waist.

repeat movement

SIN, TRESPASS, TRANSGRESSION, INIQUITY, OFFENSE (E)

This sign is a combination of BREAK and LAW and refers to an offense against the laws of God.

Formation: With both downturned "s" hands side by side in front of the chest, jerk the hands up and apart by twisting the wrists outward, Then strike the right "l" hand on the left open palm, palms facing each other.

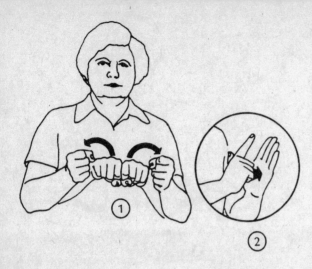

SINNER (A)

This is a combination of SIN (C) and the person marker.

Formation: With both "x" hands make simultaneous circles by moving the hands upward and outward, palms facing up near each side of the waist. Add the person marker.

SINNER (B)

This sign is a combination of SIN (B) and the person marker.

Formation: Beginning with both extended index fingers pointing toward each other in front of the body, palms facing in, move them in repeated opposite circles toward and away from each other. Add the person marker.

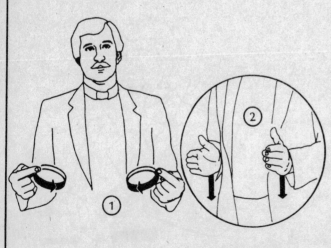

SLAVERY, CAPTIVITY, BONDAGE

The wrists seem to be bound together. This sign refers to the years of captivity of the Jews by the Egyptians.

Formation: With the base of the right "s" hand on the back of the left "s" hand, both palms facing down, move the hands in a clockwise circle in front of the waist.

repeat movement

SOCIETY

This is an initialized sign formed like CLASS and indicates a group of people sharing a similar culture.

Formation: Move both "s" hands, palms facing foward, from touching in front of the chest in a circle outward until the little fingers meet, palms facing the body.

See also CONGREGATION, DIOCESE, and ERUV for initialized signs formed in a similar manner.

SOLEMN, SILENCE, PEACEFUL

The hands move down in a natural gesture of quieting a group, as during a religious ceremony.

Formation: Cross the left "b" hand in front of the right "b" hand at the mouth, palms facing each other and fingertips pointing up. Smoothly move the hands downward and apart, ending with the palms down.

Same sign for TRANQUIL, CALM, STILL, SILENT, QUIET

SON

This sign is a combination of BOY and a modification of BABY and is used to refer to Jesus as the Son of God and the second person of the Trinity.

Formation: Bring the right "b" hand down smoothly from a saluting position on the forehead to the crook of the bent left arm, ending with both palms up.

SORROW, CONTRITION, REPENT, PENITENT, ATONEMENT, SORRY, REGRET

The movement of the sign indicates rubbing away pressure on the heart from contrition.

Formation: Rub the right "a" hand, palm facing in, over the heart in a circular motion repeatedly.

Same sign for APOLOGIZE

See also MOURN and SUFFER for signs with a related meaning.

SORROWFUL, DEJECTED, SAD (A)

The hands and countenance demonstrate a dejected and downcast posture.

Formation: Bring both loose "5" hands down in front of the face, palms facing in.

Note: The head should be slightly bowed.

Same sign for FORLORN, DOWNCAST, DESPONDENT

See also SORROW for the noun form of this sign.

SOUL, SPIRIT, SPIRITUAL

The fingers reach deep inside, the traditional location of the immortal spiritual nature of man.

Formation: Bring the fingertips of the right "f" hand, palm facing down, from inside the left "o" hand held close to the body, upward in front of the chest.

See also SPIRIT for an alternate sign.

SPIRIT, SPIRITUAL, GHOST, SOUL

The fingers seem to hold something thin and filmy, symbolic of a supernatural being such as the Holy Spirit.

Formation: Touch the thumbs and index fingers of both "f" hands to each other, right hand over left, palms facing. Draw the hands apart, lifting the right hand in front of the chest.

See also SOUL for an alternate sign.

See also HOLY GHOST for a sign with a related meaning.

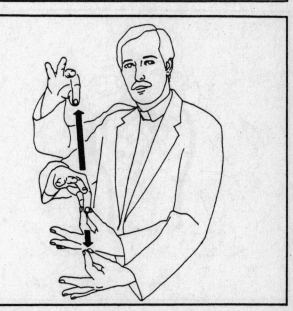

STAR

The fingers mime the twinkling rays from stars, such as the rays that led the wise men to Christ's birthplace in Bethlehem.

Formation: Brush the sides of both extended index fingers together, palms away from the body, with an alternating motion as the hands move upward.

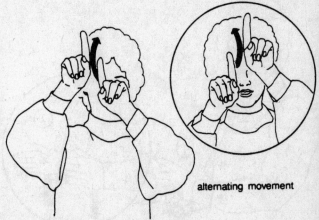

alternating movement

STATIONS OF THE CROSS

The sign is formed like several crosses and represents meditating before fourteen crosses set up to commemorate the fourteen events in the Passion of Jesus.

Formation: With the right extended index finger pointing up, palm left, hold the left extended index finger, pointing right and palm down, across it, first in front of the left shoulder and then in front of the right shoulder.

Note: The sign for FOURTEEN may be made before forming this sign.

See also WAY OF THE CROSS for a sign with a related meaning.

STATUE, IMAGE

The hands follow the form of an imaginary statue, such as those that represent religious figures.

Formation: Move the extended thumbs of both "a" hands, palms facing forward, from in front of each side of the head downward in a wavy movement to in front of the body, ending with the palms facing down.

Same sign for FIGURE, SCULPTURE

See also IDOL for an initialized sign formed in a similar manner.

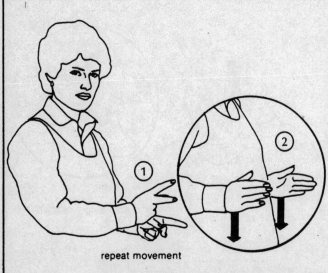

repeat movement

STEWARD

This sign is a combination of KEEP and the person marker and refers to a person who manage's God's gifts and uses them for God's glory.

Formation: Tap the little-finger side of the right "k" hand, palm left, to the index-finger side of the left "k" hand, palm right. Add the person marker.

STRAY, APOSTASY

The hands mime being diverted from the "straight and narrow," as occurs when one abandons one's religious faith.

Formation: Beginning with both extended index fingers, pointing forward with the palms down, side by side in front of the waist, move the right finger forward and off to the right at an angle.

See also BACKSLIDE for an alternate sign.

SUKKOTH, FEAST OF TABERNACLES

The hands of this initialized sign follow the shape of a hut and symbolize the eight-day festival commemorating the dwelling in huts by the Jews during their exodus through the desert.

Formation: Bring both "s" hands, palms facing foward, from near each other in front of the forehead, outward beyond each shoulder and then straight downward, ending on each side of the waist.

See also CHUPPAH for another sign formed in a similar manner.

SUFFER, SUFFERING, ENDURE, BEAR (A)

This sign is formed somewhat like PATIENCE but with a twist of the hand and indicates a sustained toleration of emotional or physical pain.

Formation: Twist the thumbnail of the right "a" hand, palm left, on the lips, ending with the palm facing toward the neck.

Same sign for TOLERATE

See also MOURN and SORROW for signs with a related meaning.

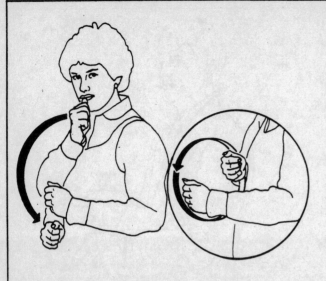

SUFFER, SUFFERING, AGONY, PASSION (B)

The hands mime deep inner turmoil, as in the Passion of Christ prior to his Crucifixion.

Formation: Bring the right "a" hand, palm left, from in front of the lips down in an arc in front of and in a complete circle around the left "a" hand, palm right.

Note: Keep the hands close to the body. The first position at the lips may be omitted.

SUNDAY SCHOOL (A)

This is an initialized sign that refers to religious instruction for children on Sunday.

Formation: Move the right "s" hand, palm facing forward, from in front of the chest to the right, knocking it forward lightly in each position.

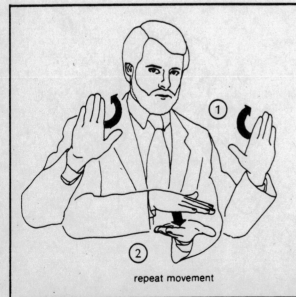

repeat movement

SUNDAY SCHOOL (B)

This sign is a combination of SUNDAY and SCHOOL.

Formation: Move both open hands, palms facing forward in front of each shoulder, in circular motions upward and outward from each other. Clap the palm of the downturned right open hand, fingers angled forward, crosswise across the upturned palm of the left open hand, with a double motion.

SYMBOL, SIGN

This initialized sign is formed like SHOW and directs attention to something in the hand.

Formation: With the thumb side of the right "s" hand, palm facing down, against the left open palm, facing right and fingers pointing up, move both hands forward a short distance.

See also REVEAL and WITNESS (B) for signs formed in a similar manner.

SYNAGOGUE, MISHKAN, SHUL

This is an initialized sign formed similar to the sign CATHEDRAL to designate a place for Jewish worship and religious instruction.

Formation: Tap the heel of the right "s" hand, palm down, on the back of the left "s" hand, palm down. Then move the right hand upward in a small arc.

See also CATHEDRAL, CHURCH, LUTHERAN (B), PARISH, PETER, and TEMPLE for other initialized signs formed in a similar manner.

TABERNACLE, MISHKAN, HOUSE

This is the sign for HOUSE and is used to specify both a Jewish temple and the case on a church alter containing the consecrated host and wine of the Eucharist.

Formation: Start with touching the index fingertips of the angled "b" hands in front of forehead, palms down. Separate, bringing the hands downward at an angle to shoulder width, then straight down, palms facing.

TAKE AWAY, SUBTRACT, REMOVE

The hands seem to sweep something away from the other hand and symbolizes Christ's redemption removing mankind's sins.

Formation: Sweep the right "claw" hand down across the upturned left hand, palms facing each other, changing into an "s" hand as it passes the left palm.

TALLITH, TALIS

The hands follow the shape of the fringed prayer shawl that has bands of blue or black and that is worn by Jewish men at prayer.

Formation: Beginning with the thumb and index fingertips of both hands on each side of the chest, palms facing the body, move them downward simultaneously.

See also BROTHER and RABBI for signs formed in a similar manner.

repeat movement

TEACH, TEACHINGS, INSTRUCTION

The hands seem to direct information at another person.

Formation: With the thumbs touching the fingertips of both hands, palms facing forward, move the hands forward in front of each side of the chest with a short deliberate double motion.

Note: INSTRUCTION may be initialized.

TEMPLE, SHUL

This is an initialized sign formed like CHURCH and signifies buildings dedicated to the worship of God, particularly in the Jewish religion.

Formation: Tap the heel of the right "t" hand, palm down, on the back of the left "s" hand, palm down.

See also CATHEDRAL, CHURCH, LUTHERAN (B), PARISH, PETER, and SYNAGOGUE for other initialized signs formed in a similar manner.

repeat movement

TEMPT, TEMPTATION

The hand taps on the elbow to divert attention, as when a person is enticed to do an immoral act, often with the promise of earthly rewards.

Formation: Tap the elbow of the bent left arm with the index fingertip of the right "x" hand.

repeat movement

TESTAMENT

This initialized sign is formed like LAW and denotes either of the two main divisions of the Bible.

Formation: Move the index-finger side of the right "t" hand, palm facing left, across the left open palm, facing forward and fingers pointing up, touching first at the fingers and then at the heel.

See also COMMANDMENTS, HALACHA (A), LAW (B), and MOSES for other initialized signs formed in a similar manner.

See also NEW TESTAMENT and OLD TESTAMENT for variations of this sign.

repeat movement

TESTIMONY, TESTIFY, WITNESS, SERMON (A)

The hand follows the gesture often used when speaking from a lectern, as when giving a public affirmation of one's faith.

Formation: Shake the open hand at shoulder level, palm left, forward and back repeatedly by twisting the wrist.

Same sign for LECTURE, PRESENT

See also BEHOLD for the verb forms of WITNESS and PREACH for an alternate sign for SERMON.

repeat movement

TESTIMONY, TESTIFY (B)

This is an initialized sign and refers to a declaration regarding a religious experience.

Formation: Shake the right "t" hand at shoulder level, palm left, forward and back repeatedly by twisting the wrist.

See also PREACH for a sign formed in a similar manner.

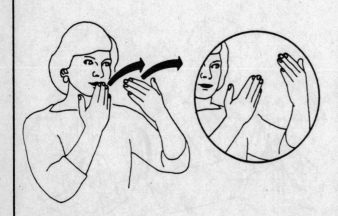

THANKFUL, THANKS, GRATEFUL, GRATITUDE

The hands bring words of gratitude from the mouth upward toward God.

Formation: Beginning with the right open hand near the mouth and the left open hand slightly forward, both palms facing in, move the hands forward and upward a short distance.

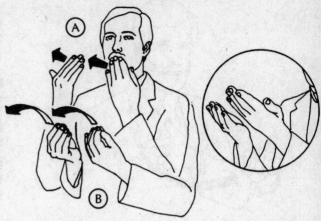

THANKSGIVING

This sign is a combination of THANKS and GIVE and refers to an expression of gratitude to God.

Formation: Beginning with the right open hand near the mouth and the left open hand slightly forward, both palms facing in, move the hands forward and upward a short distance. Then with the thumbs and fingertips of each hand touching, palms facing up, move both hands forward and upward from in front of the chest while opening into "5" hands.

THEE, THOU

This directional sign is a natural gesture for the second-person pronoun when it is used to refer to God.

Formation: Move the right open hand from above the right shoulder a short distance upward, palm angled left and fingertips pointing up.

See also THINE for the possessive pronoun referring to God.

THEOLOGY (A)

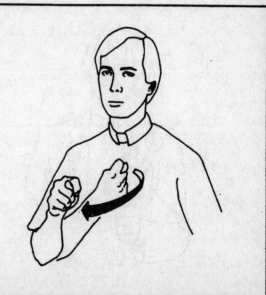

This is an initialized sign formed like RELIGION and refers to a formalized body of opinions concerning God and man's relationship with God.

Formation: Touch the fingertips of the right "t" hand to the left side of the chest, palm facing the body. Then move the "t" smoothly down while twisting the wrist outward, ending with the palm facing left.

See also RELIGION for another initialized sign with a related meaning formed in a similar manner.

173

THEOLOGY (B)

This is an initialized sign formed like RE-LIGION and refers to the study of the nature of God and religious truth.

Formation: Touch the palm side of the right "l" hand to the left side of the chest. Then move the right hand smoothly forward in an arc while changing into a "t" hand, palm facing down.

See also RELIGION for another initialized sign with a related meaning formed in a similar manner.

THINE, THY

This is a directional sign toward God using the open palm, which is the sign formation used for possessive pronouns in American Sign Language.

Formation: Move the right open hand from above the right shoulder a short distance upward, palm angled upward and fingertips pointing toward the back of the head.

See also THEE for the second-person pronoun referring to God.

TITHE

This sign is a combination of ONE and TEN formed as a fraction and indicates the payment of one-tenth of one's income to God through the support of a church.

Formation: Hold the right extended index finger pointing upward in front of the chest, palm facing forward. Then lower the hand a few inches while twisting the wrist and changing to an "a" hand, palm left and thumb extended up.

TONGUE, LANGUAGE (A)

This is an intialized sign formed like SEN-TENCE and refers to a medium for the transmission of communication.

Formation: Beginning with the thumbs of both downturned "l" hands touching in front of the waist, bring them apart in an arc by flipping the wrists outward.

TONGUE, SPEAKING IN TONGUES (B)

This sign is a combination of TELL and SPEAK and refers to the gift of the Holy Spirit to declare the gospel to all people.

Formation: Touch the extended right index finger to the lips, palm facing in. Then beginning both "4" hands, right hand near the mouth, palm left, and left hand out somewhat, palm right. Move both hands forward repeatedly with short movements while wiggling the fingers.

See also CHARISMATIC (A) (B) and PENTECOST for signs with a related meaning.

TORAH, SCROLL (A)

The hands unroll an imaginary scroll and refers to the parchment scroll on which the Pentateuch is written and used during services in a synagogue.

Formation: Move both "s" hands from near each other in front of the waist, palms facing each other, away from each other by twisting the wrists up and down.

repeat movement

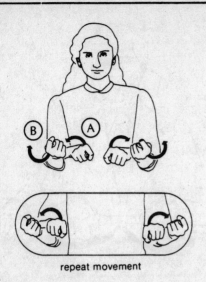

TORAH (B)

The hands in this initialized sign seem to unroll a scroll.

Formation: Move both "t" hands from near each other in front of the waist, palms facing down, away from each other by twisting the wrists up and down.

repeat movement

TRADITION

This initialized sign is formed like ANCESTORS with the hands moving from a location that indicates the past in American Sign Language to the present and symbolizes the handing down of unwritten religious precepts from generation to generation.

Formation: Move the right and left "t" hands over each other forward from in front of the right shoulder, ending in front of the waist, palms facing the body.

TRANSLATE, TRANSLATION

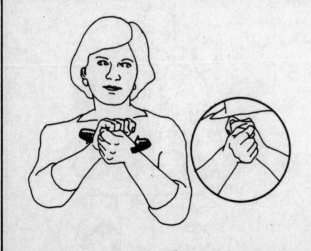

The sign is formed like CHANGE and indicates the process of expressing text into another language while retaining its original sense, as in translations of the Bible.

Formation: With the palms of both "t" hands facing each other and hands held together at angles with each other, twist the wrists in opposite directions with alternative movements toward and away from the body.

See also: CONVERT, INTERPRET, and REPENT for other signs formed in a similar manner.

TRIBULATION, TROUBLE

This is an initialized sign formed like TROUBLE and refers to great distress or suffering.

Formation: With an alternative movement bring both "t" hands, palms facing each other, from the forehead level downward across the face several times.

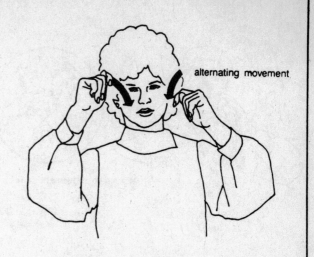

alternating movement

TRINITY

This sign is combination of THREE and ONE. The movement shows the "three" being changed or integrated into "one" and symbolizes the union of three divine figures—Father, Son, and Holy Spirit—in one godhead.

Formation: With the back of the right "3" hand resting in the palm of the left open hand, both palms toward the chest, pull the right hand down behind the left hand while changing into a "1" hand, which then moves in a big arc in front of the left hand, right index finger pointing straight up and palm toward the body.

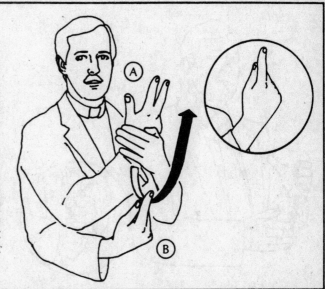

TRIUMPH, TRIUMPHANT, ATTAIN, FINALLY

This sign is a natural gesture for expressing success.

Formation: Starting with both index fingers pointing toward each other in front of the chest, both palms facing the body, twist the wrists outward, ending with the index fingers pointing upward, palms forward.

Same sign for SUCCEED, SUCCESS, SUCCESSFUL, AT LAST

See also VICTORY and CELEBRATE for signs with a related meaning.

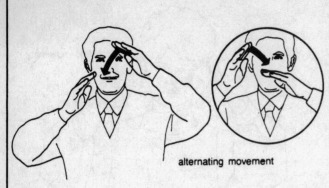

alternating movement

TROUBLE, CARE, WORRY

The hands represent that things are coming from all sides causing worry.

Formation: With an alternating movement bring both "b" hands, palms facing down, from the forehead level downward across the face several times.

Same sign for CONCERN

See also TRIBULATION for an initialized sign with a related meaning formed in a similar manner.

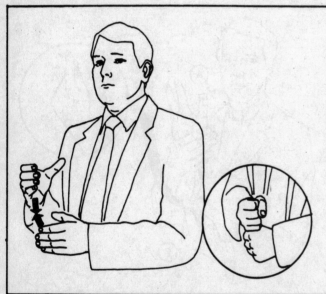

TRUST, CONFIDENCE

The hands seem to grab hold of something and indicates confidence or reliance on something unseen.

Formation: Hold the right "c" hand a few inches above the left "c" hand, palms facing each other, slightly away from the body. Bring the hands together and toward the body, changing them into "s" hands as they move.

See also FAITH (A) for an alternate sign.

TRUTH, HONEST, HONESTY (A)

This is an initialized sign that indicates presenting something in a straightforward and honest way.

Formation: Move the right "h" hand, palm left and fingers pointing forward, across the upturned left palm from the heel outward toward the fingertips.

TRUTH, TRULY (B)

This sign is a combination of TRUE and HONEST and indicates that something that is said is factual.

Formation: Bring the right extended index finger, palm left, forward from the mouth a short distance. Then push the fingertips of the right "h" hand, palm left, across the upturned left palm, from the heel outward toward the fingertips.

See also VERILY for a sign with a similar meaning.

TZEDAKAH

This sign is a combination of MONEY and a gesture that seems to put money into a container and refers to the traditional acts of charity performed by observant Jews.

Formation: Tap the back of the upturned flattened "o" right hand on the palm of the upturned open left hand. Then insert the thumb and index fingertip of the right "f" hand into the thumb-side opening of the left "o" hand with a repeated motion.

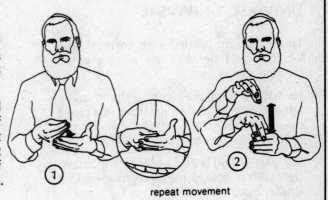

repeat movement

UNITE, JOIN, AFFILIATE, BELONG

The hands come together and intertwine as a symbol of coming together for a common purpose or interest.

Formation: Beginning with both "c" hands apart in front of the chest, palms facing each other, bring them to each other, intersecting the touching thumbtip and index fingertip of each hand with the other.

See also MEMBER (B) for a sign with a related meaning.

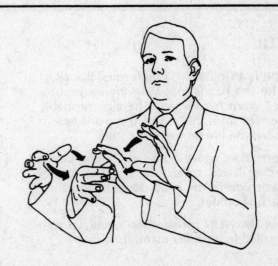

UNITY, COMMUNION OF SAINTS, UNIVERSAL, CATHOLIC

This sign is a modification of UNITE and indicates the common religious faith that unites Christians.

Formation: With the thumbtip and index fingertip of each hand touching and intersecting with the other hand, palms facing, move the hands in a flat circle in front of the body.

See also COMMUNION OF SAINTS (A) for an alternate sign.

UNIVERSE, UNIVERSAL

This is an initialized sign formed like WORLD and signifies the sphere of all created things.

Formation: Bring the right "u" hand, palm left and fingers angled upward, in a circle over and around the left "u" hand, palm right and fingers forward.

See also WORLD for another initialized sign with a related meaning formed in a similar manner.

VEIL

This is an initialized sign formed like NUN with the hands following the shape of a veil worn by women. The sign probably derives from the use of the word *veil* to mean the life or vows of a nun.

Formation: Move both "v" hands, palms facing back, from touching the top of each side of the head down to touching each shoulder.

See also NUN for another initialized sign formed in a similar manner.

VERILY, TRULY, INDEED

The sign indicates speaking straight forwardly with factual accuracy.

Formation: Move the side of the extended right index finger up against the lips and outward in an arc.

Same sign for ACTUALLY, CERTAINLY, REALLY, SURELY

See also TRUTH for a sign with a related meaning.

VERSE

The fingers seem to measure out a short passage such as one of the numbered subdivisions of a chapter in a Bible.

Formation: Move the right "g" fingertips, palm facing down, across the upturned left palm from the base to the fingertips.

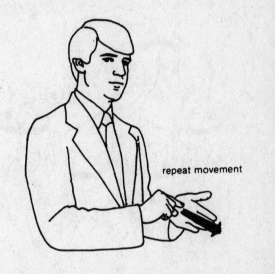

repeat movement

VESPERS

The sign is a combination of NIGHT and PRAY and refers to worship or prayers held in the late afternoon or evening.

Formation: Tap the wrist of the bent open right hand, palm down, on the top of the wrist of the downturned left arm, extended across the body to the right. Then with both open hands, palms against each other and fingers angled up and forward, move the hands inward and downward slightly.

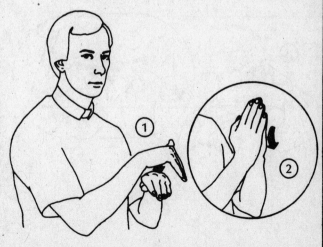

VESTMENTS

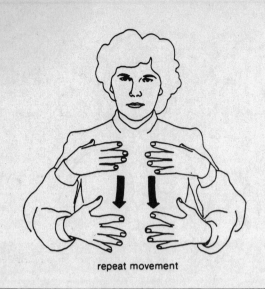

repeat movement

The hands indicate the location of the ritual robes worn by the clergy during church services.

Formation: Starting with the thumbtips of both "5" hands, palms toward the body on the upper part of each side of the chest, sweep the thumbs downward repeatedly.

See also ROBE for a sign with a related meaning.

VICTORY

This initialized sign is formed like PRAISE and CELEBRATE and symbolizes the final defeat of an enemy, such as Satan.

Formation: Pat the palms of both hands together, fingers pointing up. Then make small circles above either shoulder with both "v" hands, palms facing toward the head.

See also ALLELUIA and CELEBRATE for signs formed in a similar manner.

VISION (A)

This sign is a combination of a modification of FAITH and a gesture of shock or surprise and indicates the appearance of a mental image of a supernatural being.

Formation: Move the right extended index finger from the forehead smoothly down, changing into an "s" hand, meeting the left "s" hand in front of the chest, both palms facing down. Then sharply pull the hands apart, opening into curved "5" hands near each side of the head, palms facing each other.

VISION (B)

The fingers represent the eyes looking past the horizon into the future.

Formation: Move the fingertips of the right "v" hand, palm down and fingers pointing forward, from in front of the eyes downward and forward under the left flat hand which is held, palm down, in front of the chest.

See also PROPHECY for another sign with a related meaning formed in a similar manner.

VOCATION (A)

This is an initialized sign formed like WORK and refers to the urge or pre-disposition to work in a religious field.

Formation: Tap the base of the right "v" hand, palm facing forward, on the back of the downturned left "s" hand with a double motion.

See also CALL (A) for an alternate sign.

repeat movement

VOCATION, WORK (B)

This is the sign WORK and refers to a calling to undertake a religious career.

Formation: Tap the base of the right "s" hand, palm facing down, on the back of the downturned left "s" hand with a double movement.

Same sign for EMPLOYMENT

See also CALL (A) for an alternate sign.

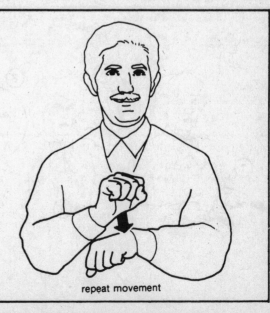

repeat movement

184

VOW, PROMISE (A)

This sign is a combination of TRUE and a natural gesture indicating a promise to tell the truth. This sign is used to refer to a solemn promise to live and act in accordance with the prescriptions of a religious body.

Formation: Bring the extended right index finger, palm left, out from the lips, changing to an open hand, palm forward, with the right bent elbow resting on the back of the downturned left hand.

Same sign for SWEAR, OATH, LOYAL, PLEDGE

VOW, PROMISE (B)

This is an initialized form of VOW (A) and indicates a solemn promise.

Formation: Bring the extended right index finger, palm left, out from the lips changing to a "v" hand, ending with the base of the right "v" hand against the index-finger side of the downturned left "b" hand.

WAY OF THE CROSS

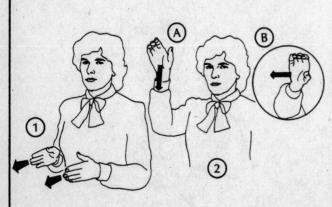

This sign is a combination of WAY and CROSS and refers to the route Christ followed from his trial to his crucifixion.

Formation: Move both open hands, palms facing each other and fingers pointing forward, parallel to each other forward in front of the waist. Then move the right "c" hand, palm facing forward, first down from above the right side of the head to the right side of the body, then from left to right in front of the right shoulder.

WEDDING

The sign shows bringing hands together, symbolizing the union of two lives during a wedding cermony.

Formation: With the "5" hands hanging down from bent wrists, swing them toward each other and grasp the fingers of the left hand with the right fingers.

See also MARRIAGE for a sign with a related meaning.

WICKED

repeat movement

This sign is DEVIL repeated and refers to something very evil.

Formation: With the thumbs of both "3" hands touching the temples, palms facing forward, crook the extended index and middle fingers repeatedly.

See also BAD, DEVIL, and EVIL for signs with related meanings.

WILDERNESS, DESERT

The sign is a combination of DRY and LAND and refers to the barren regions of the Holy Land.

Formation: Draw the right "x" index finger, palm down, across the chin from left to right. Then rub the thumbs of both hands across the fingertips from the little finger to the index finger, palms facing up. Flip the hands over and open them into both downturned "5" hands while pushing them forward and outward, fingers pointing forward.

WILL, GOD'S WILL

This is an initialized sign formed like LAW and refers to God's commandments to mankind.

Formation: Strike the index-finger side of the right "w" hand, palm facing forward, against the left open hand, palm facing right.

See also DESIRE (A) for an alternate sign.

repeat movement

WINE

This is an initialized sign.

Formation: Stroke the thumb of the right "w" hand in small circles on the right cheek, palm toward the cheek.

Note: The palm may face forward and the side of the index finger brush in circles on the cheek.

repeat movement

WISDOM, WISE

The motion of the hand shows deep thinking.

Formation: Shake the right "x" index finger, pointing downward with the palm left, up and down in front of the forehead.

WITNESS (A)

This is an initialized sign that signifies seeing something and presenting it for view as evidence.

Formation: Move the index finger of the right "w" hand from touching near the right eye down to touch the left open palm, facing right.

See also PROOF for a sign with a related meaning formed in a similar manner.

WITNESS (B)

This is an initialized sign like SHOW and indicates the idea of presenting evidence.

Formation: With the index finger of the right "w" hand, palm left, touching the open left palm, facing forward, jab both hands forward with a repeated motion.

See also REVEAL and SYMBOL for signs formed in a similar manner.

repeat movement

WONDER, WONDERFUL, MARVEL

This sign is a natural gesture for exclaiming delight.

Formation: Pat the air repeatedly with both "5" hands, palms facing forward above each shoulder.

Same sign for TERRIFIC, GREAT, FANTASTIC, MARVELOUS, GRAND

See also PONDER for the verb form of this sign and MIRACLE for an alternate sign for MARVEL.

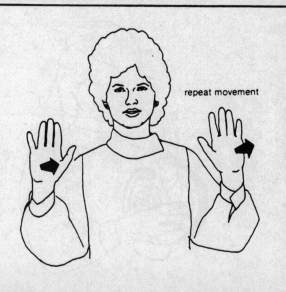

repeat movement

repeat movement

WORD

The fingers demonstrate a small portion of a sentence. This sign is used to refer to the Word of God as presented in the Scriptures.

Formation: Touch the tips of right thumb and index finger, palm left, to the extended left index finger, palm right.

repeat movement

WORKS, DEEDS, DO

This is the sign for DO and signifies moral or righteous actions.

Formation: Swing both downturned "c" hands back and forth in opposite directions to and from each other in front of the waist.

Same sign for ACT, ACTION

See also MITZVAH for an initialized sign formed in a similar manner.

WORLD

This is an initialized sign that traces the shape of the globe.

Formation: Bring the right "w" hand, palm left and fingers forward, in a circle over and around the left "w" hand, palm right and fingers forward.

See also UNIVERSE for another initialized sign with a related meaning formed in a similar manner.

WORSHIP, ADORE, ADORATION, AMEN, PIOUS, DEVOUT

The hands mime a worshipful pose and show reverence for a diety.

Formation: Cup the fingers of the right hand over the left "a" hand, palms downward. Move the hands upward in an arc toward the body.

See also PRAY for an alternate sign.

WORTHY, DESERVE

The hands seem to bring something of value or worth to the top of the pile for examination or recognition.

Formation: Beginning with both "f" hands in front of the body, little fingers touching the palms up, bring the hands upward in two large arcs away from each other, ending with the thumbs touching and the palms facing down.

Same sign for WORTH, VALUE, VALUABLE, IMPORTANT; VALUE and VALUABLE are sometimes initialized.

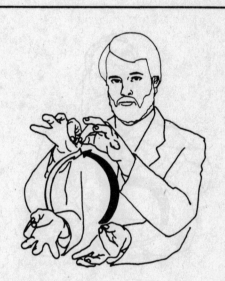

WRONG, MISTAKE, ERROR

Formation: Tap the chin with the middle fingers of the right "y" hand, palm facing the body.

repeat movement

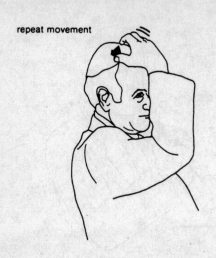

repeat movement

YARMULKE, KIPAH, SKULLCAP

The hand demonstrates the shape of the traditional headcovering worn by Jewish males.

Formation: Tap the fingertips of the right "c" hand, palm down, on top of the head with a double motion.

YESHIVA (A)

This initialized sign is formed like COLLEGE and refers to an institute of talmudic learning.

Formation: Bring the downturned right "y" hand from on the upturned left palm upward in an arc.

See also SEMINARY for another sign formed in a similar manner.

repeat movement

YESHIVA (B)

This is an initialized sign.

Formation: Move the right "y" hand, palm facing out, in a small clockwise circle near the right shoulder.

YOM KIPPUR, DAY OF ATONEMENT (A)

The sign is a combination of DAY and SORROW.

Formation: Place the elbow of the bent right arm, hand held straight up, palm left, on the downturned left hand. Move the extended right index finger downward toward the left elbow keeping the right elbow in place. Then rub the "a" hand, palm facing in, over the heart in a circular motion repeatedly.

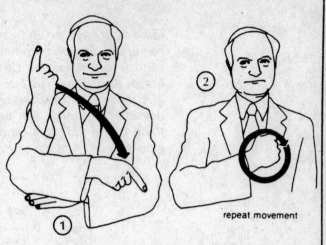

repeat movement

YOM KIPPUR, DAY OF ATONEMENT, FAST (B)

The hand beats on the chest as a sign of sorrow and refers to the Jewish holiday on which fasting and prayer for the atonement of sins is prescribed.

Formation: Knock the palm side of the right "a" hand rapidly against the left side of the chest.

See also FRUM for a sign formed in a similar manner.

repeat movement

ZIZITH, TSITSITH

The fingers seem to pull on the tassels of thread, reminders of God's commandments, located on the four corners of prayer aprons worn by Jewish males.

Formation: With the fingertips of both "g" hands touching each hip, palms facing the body, bring the hands down and out while pinching the thumb and index fingers together as the hands move.

repeat movement

The Lord's Prayer

Our Father, who art in heaven. Hallowed be Thy name. Thy kingdom come. Thy will be done on earth as it is in heaven. Give us this day our daily bread. And forgive us our trespasses, as we forgive those who trespass against us. And lead us not into temptation, but deliver us from evil. For thine is the kingdom, and the power, and the glory forever. Amen.

Matthew 6

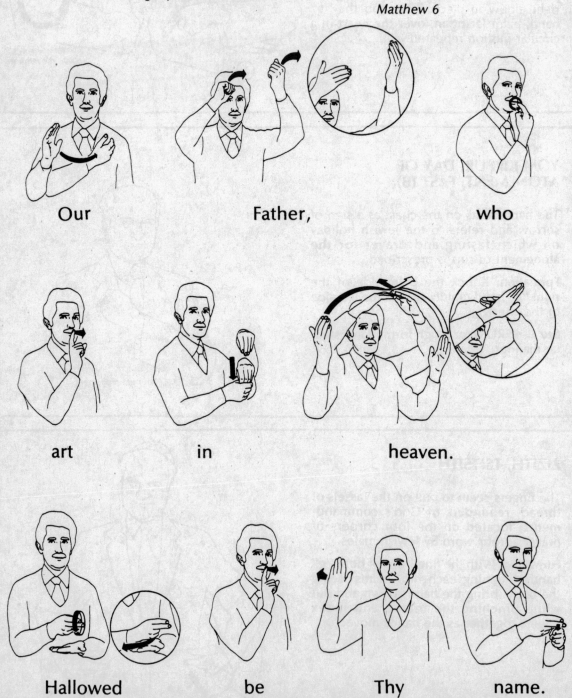

Our Father, who

art in heaven.

Hallowed be Thy name.

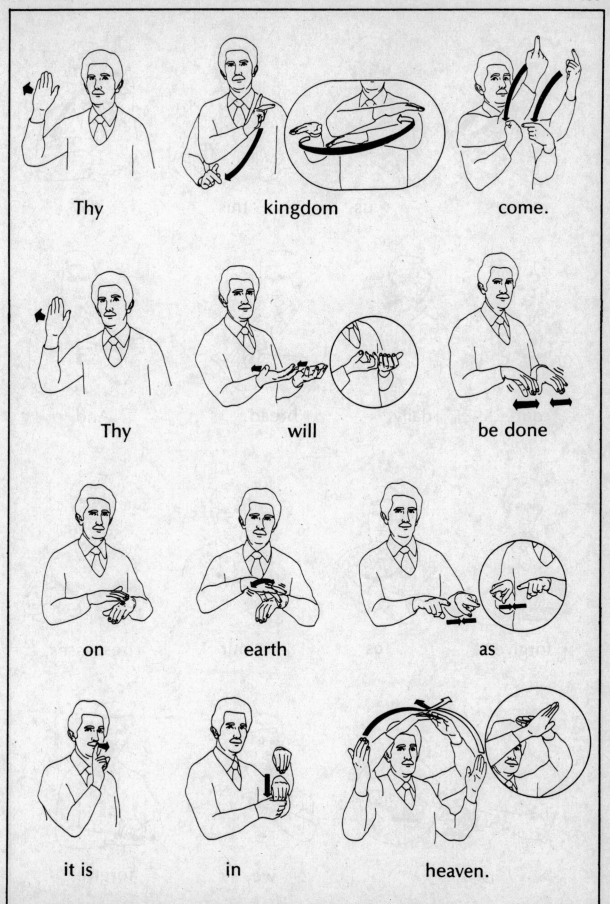

Thy   kingdom   come.

Thy   will   be done

on   earth   as

it is   in   heaven.

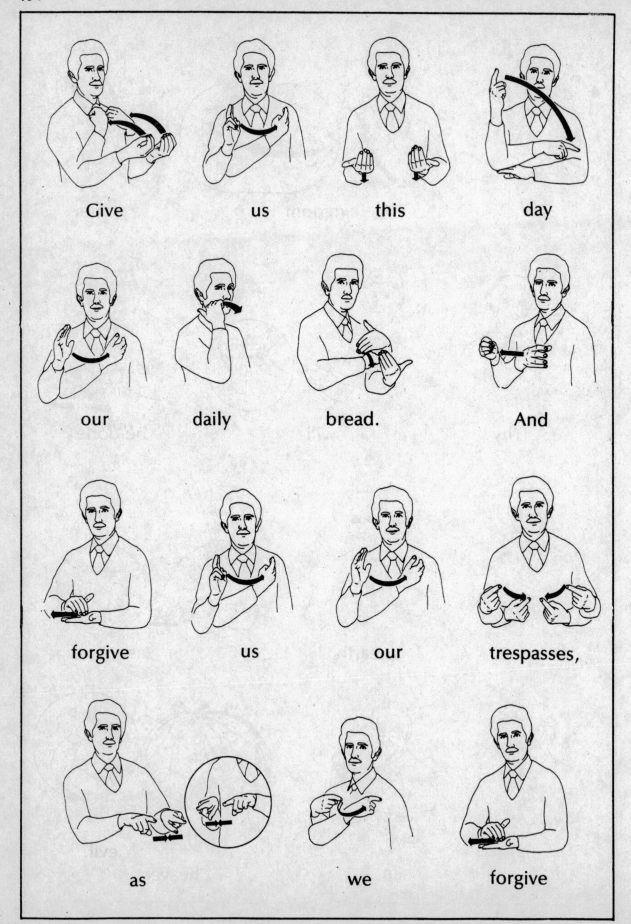

Give	us	this	day
our	daily	bread.	And
forgive	us	our	trespasses,
as		we	forgive

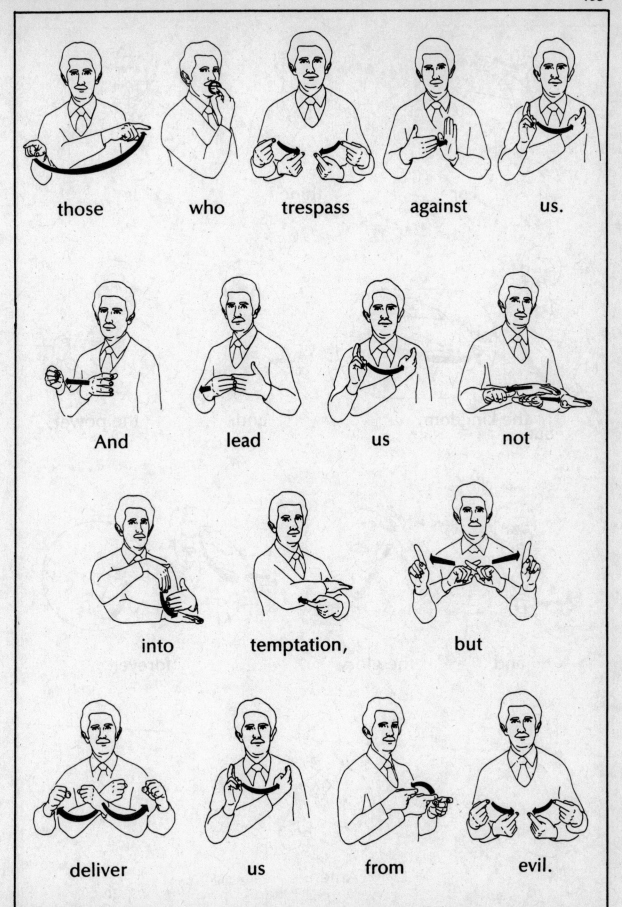

those   who   trespass   against   us.

And   lead   us   not

into   temptation,   but

deliver   us   from   evil.

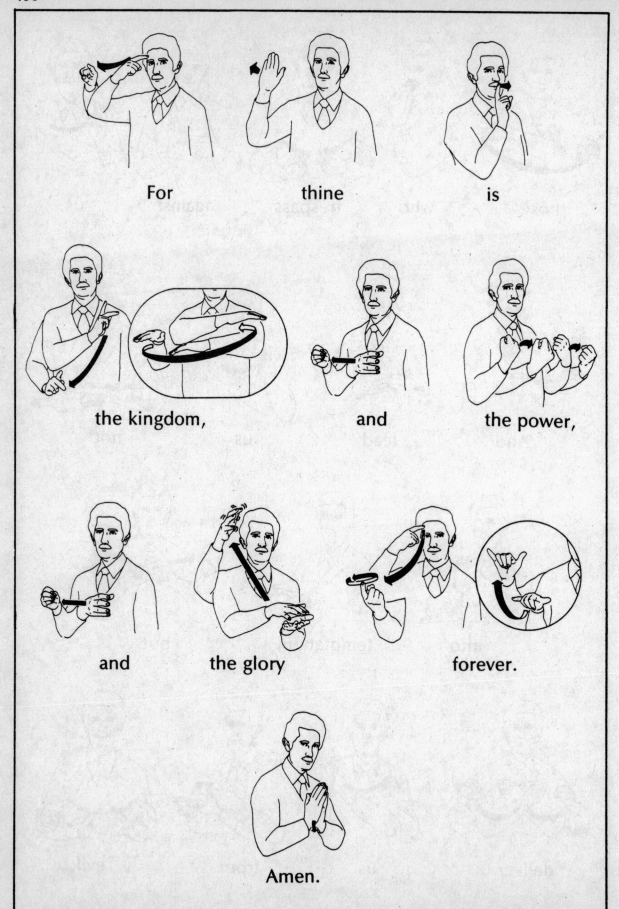

For   thine   is

the kingdom,   and   the power,

and   the glory   forever.

Amen.

Gloria Patri

*Glory to the Father, and to the Son, and to the
Holy Spirit; as it was in the beginning, is now, and
will be forever. Amen.*

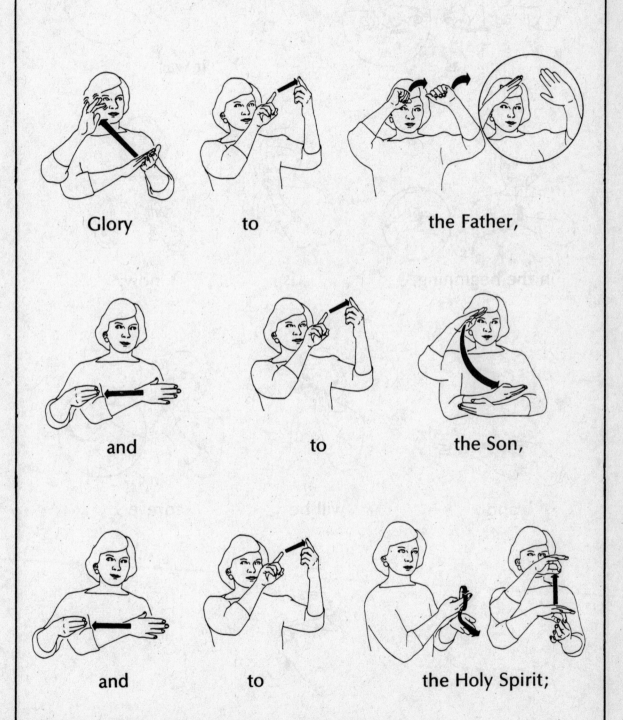

Glory   to   the Father,

and   to   the Son,

and   to   the Holy Spirit;

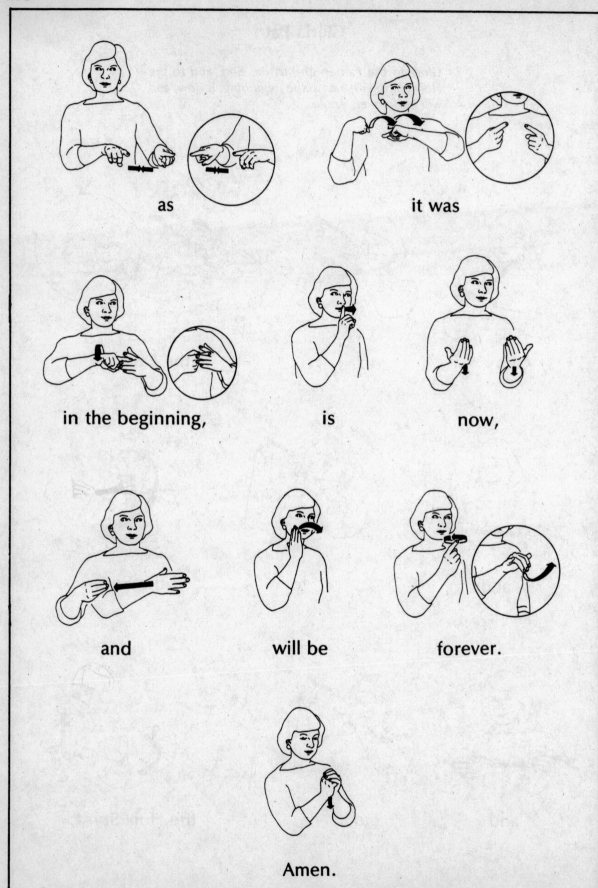

as   it was

in the beginning,   is   now,

and   will be   forever.

Amen.

Prayer for Grace

Let the words of my mouth and the meditation of my heart be acceptable in your sight, O Lord, my strength and my Redeemer.

Psalm 19:14

Let

the words

of

my

mouth

and

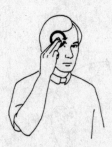

the meditation

of

my

heart

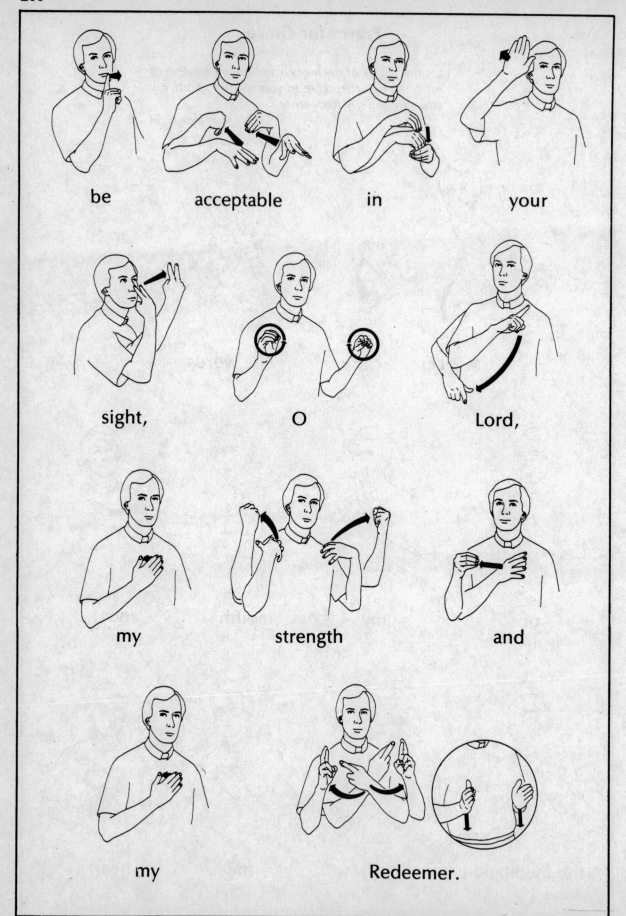

be acceptable in your

sight, O Lord,

my strength and

my Redeemer.

Giving of Thanks

O give thanks unto the Lord, for he is good, for His mercy endureth forever. Amen.

Psalm 106:1

O   give   thanks unto

the Lord,   for   he   is

good,   for   His mercy

endureth   forever.

The Shema

Hear, O Israel, the Lord is our God. The Lord is One.

Hear,   O Israel,

the Lord   is   our   God.

The Lord   is   One.

Blessing Over the Sabbath Candles

Blessed are you, O Lord our God, King of the universe, who has sanctified us with his commandments and commanded us to kindle the Sabbath lights.

Blessed   **are**   **you,**

O Lord   **our**   **God,**

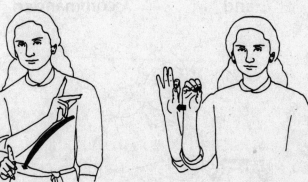

King   **of**   **the universe,**

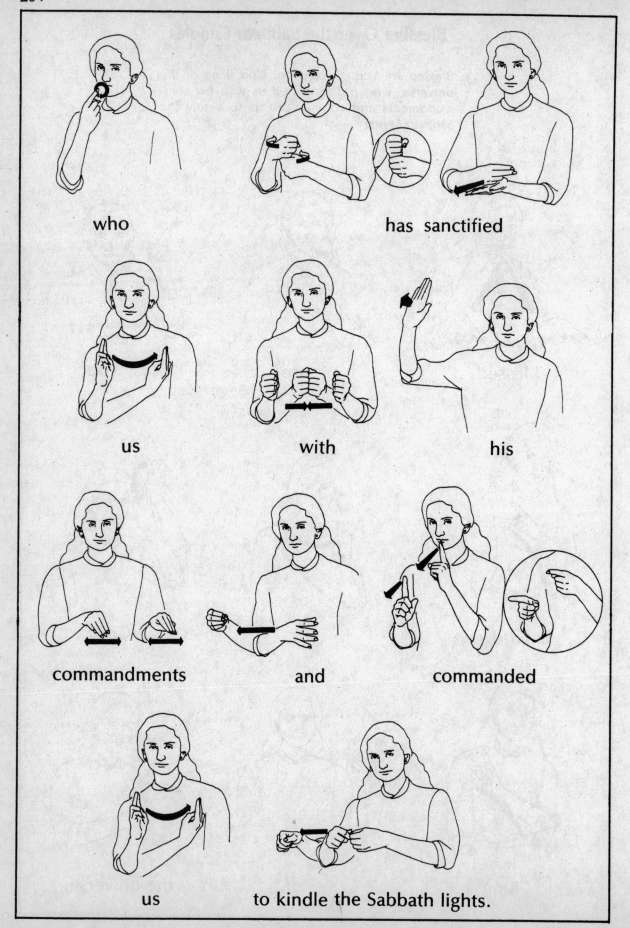

who

has sanctified

us

with

his

commandments

and

commanded

us

to kindle the Sabbath lights.

205

The Kiddush

*Blessed are you, O Lord our God, King of the
universe, who created the fruit of the vine.*

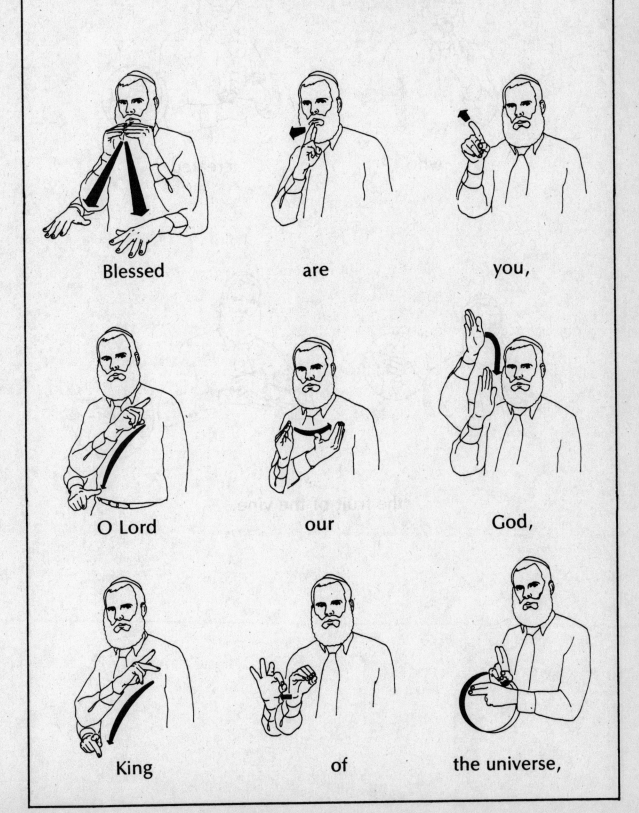

Blessed are you,

O Lord our God,

King of the universe,

who   created

the fruit of the vine.

Blessing Over Bread

Blessed are you, O Lord our God, King of the universe, who brings forth bread from the earth.

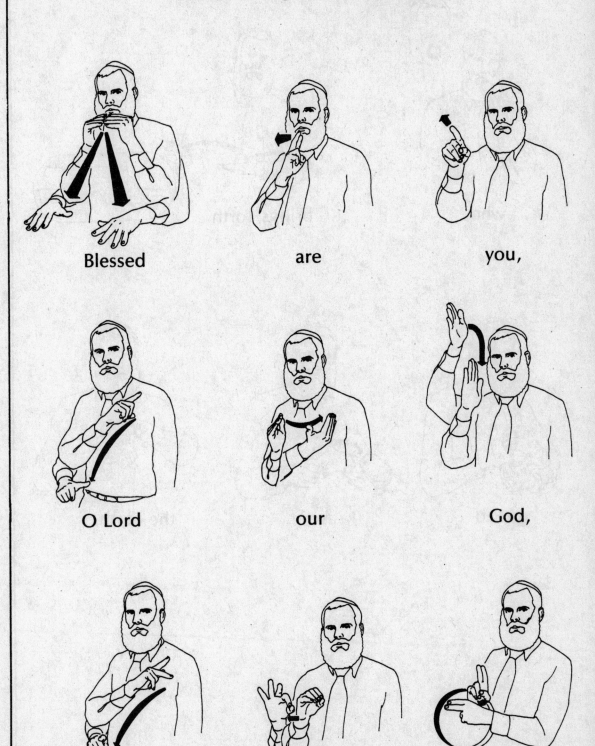

Blessed

are

you,

O Lord

our

God,

King

of

the universe,

who

brings forth

bread

from

the earth.

Index

214